The Language
of Behavior

The Language of Behavior

A Framework to Elevate Student Success

Joshua Stamper
and Charle Peck

ConnectEDD Publishing
Hanover, Pennsylvania

Copyright © 2025 by Joshua Stamper and Charle Peck

All rights reserved. No part of this publication may be reproduced, distributed, or transmitted in any form or by any means, including photocopying, recording, or other electronic or mechanical methods, without the prior written permission of the publisher, except in the case of brief quotations embodied in critical reviews and certain other noncommercial uses permitted by copyright law. For permission requests, contact the publisher at: info@connecteddpublishing.com

This publication is available at discount pricing when purchased in quantity for educational purposes, promotions, or fundraisers. For inquiries and details, contact the publisher at: info@connecteddpublishing.com

Published by ConnectEDD Publishing LLC
Hanover, PA
www.connecteddpublishing.com

Cover Design: Kheila Casas

The Language of Behavior. —1st ed. Paperback
ISBN: 979-8-9918506-2-9

Praise for *The Language of Behavior*

In their new book, *The Language of Behavior*, Joshua Stamper and Charle Peck effectively accomplish something that is very difficult to do in writing for educators: they provide practical, real-world examples of how educators can effectively correct or pre-emptively impact student behaviors in positive ways. Their strategies make the student the center of the equation but not separate from the equation. The book emphasizes the importance of staff consistency so students are not confused and do not have to constantly adjust their behaviors to meet adult needs. Listening to and working with students in new and different ways are keys to understanding this dynamic. I highly recommend this book for team book studies, whether among teachers, teachers with administrators, or administrative teams. The suggestions and exercises are practical, and many ideas can be quickly implemented.

—Tim Hanner | Retired Superintendent, Founder/Owner Hanner Educational Enterprises, CoFounder/Owner Administrators Roundtable Network

I appreciate that *The Language of Behavior* emphasizes understanding over punishment and offers actionable strategies to address the root causes of student behavior. By equipping educators with tools to build trust and create meaningful connections, this book is a step toward transforming schools into environments where every student can thrive.

—Mina Jo Blazy, PhD | Director of Continuous Improvement, Program Evaluation, Data, and Assessment

As a teacher-leader in my school building, I needed a framework to help beginning teachers strengthen their classroom culture through appropriate, student-centered responses to misbehavior. *The Language of Behavior* by Charle Peck and Joshua Stamper provides a deep understanding of student behavior through personal reflection and self-improvement.

Peck and Stamper lay out three easy-to-follow and tenets that will transform your classroom management practices and strengthen your relationships and resolve with students. Stop the Band-aid fixes that won't last and move towards long-term solutions to elevate student academic and social-emotional success with The *Language of Behavior*.

> —David C. James | 7th Grade Teacher-Leader; Cabarrus County Schools, North Carolina

I wholeheartedly recommend this book. There are concepts the veteran and new teacher can use is their classrooms tomorrow. Most important, this goes beyond classroom management and delves into the reasons why and how students respond in your classroom. This book should be required reading for new and experienced teachers as it answers questions about student behavior we all have throughout our careers. New teachers can create healthy and impactful strategies at the start of their career and veterans can reflect on their own practices and grow, too.

> —Ben Lusk | Former District Administrator: Curriculum, Professional Development, Federal Grants, Assessment, Teacher Evaluation

It is undeniable that traditional responses to student misbehavior are broken, often alienating and isolating many of our most fragile students. As Peck and Stamper explain, student misbehavior is a cry for help, and expression to be *seen*. When educators embrace this truth, we are far more likely to respond with empathy and remove our "self" in our response to student behavior. The authors gracefully illuminate our path forward, equipping educators with the understanding, and the tools, to recognize that discipline is actually another opportunity to teach our children. *The Language of Behavior* is a must read for every educator, and parent, on the planet committed to *seeing* every child and setting them up for success

> —Mitch Weathers | Founder and CEO of Organized Binder, Author

The Language of Behavior is a transformative guide for educators seeking to redefine their approach to student behavior. Joshua Stamper and Charle Peck masterfully blend empathy, practicality, and research-informed strategies to create an actionable and inspiring framework. Through relatable anecdotes and clear, step-by-step guidance, they empower readers to move beyond traditional methods and embrace a trauma-informed, restorative approach that fosters trust, growth, and meaningful connections. This book is not just a resource—it's a call to action for all educators to see behavior as a language to be understood. Emphasizing the importance of creating safe, supportive environments, *The Language of Behavior* equips educators with the tools to help students thrive academically, emotionally, and socially. It is essential reading for anyone who believes in the power of relationships and is committed to helping students succeed in every facet of their lives.

—Evan Robb | Principal, Author, Speaker

The Language of Behavior is a game-changing resource for educators and leaders seeking to truly understand and address student behavior. Charle Peck and Joshua Stamper masterfully combine therapeutic insight with practical school leadership strategies, offering a roadmap to create supportive, relationship-driven environments where students and teachers can thrive. From decoding behavior to implementing innovative solutions like the push-in model, this book equips readers with the tools to transform their classrooms and schools. Charle and Josh's collaboration brings depth, wisdom, and actionable steps that will resonate with anyone passionate about improving education. This is more than a book—it's a brilliant guide to building connection, trust, and long-lasting change.

—Darrin Peppard, EdD | Educator, Author, Speaker,
   & Leadership Expert

The Language of Behavior is a must-read for all educators seeking to create a more empathetic and supportive classroom environment. By offering relatable stories and actionable advice, this book provides a digestible, and approachable, format to understanding and addressing student behavior. It encourages educators to look beyond surface-level actions, reflect on their own mindset, and strengthen their ability to connect with and support students effectively across all grade levels.

—Kim Gameroz | Founder and CEO of Teaching Inside Out® and SELebrate Good Times®

The Language of Behavior offers a paradigm-shifting framework that redefines traditional discipline through a lens of empathy, trust, and intentionality. Grounded in research and practical application, this essential guide transforms behavior challenges into teachable moments while modeling empathy to foster a stronger, more compassionate school culture, an approach urgently needed in schools across the nation. This is a total game-changer. Forget outdated discipline tactics; this guide is all about turning behavior issues into real opportunities for connection and growth. Packed with tools to model empathy and build trust, it's the blueprint for creating a compassionate school culture every school in the nation should be implementing.

—Eric Skanson, Ed. D | School Pro K12 Owner & Founder, Innovative Charter School Director, 2019 National Distinguished Principal

I really enjoyed how the research-based strategies are so easy to implement if leaders make the time for educators to look, listen, learn, and act in the best interests of our kids. The best part from my lens as a former teacher, building principal, and as a current superintendent was the real-life scenarios used to educate, advocate, and to bring heightened awareness to how adult behavior can make or break a scholar's ability to not only be successful in school but also in life. I will form

R.A.T.S at every building to work proactively to meet the educational, psychological, and mental health needs of all students and their families. I will also use this book as a professional learning guide/tool for adults, including bus drivers, cafeteria workers, custodians, as well as professional educational staff, school and division leaders. The Language of Behavior is the playbook for everyone and anyone involved in successfully educating our children.

—Dr. Herb Monroe | Superintendent Surry County Public Schools, Motivational Speaker

In this informative book, Josh and Charle explore how teacher actions and interactions in the classroom influence student behavior. By taking a curious stance and seeking to understand our students, we can all build strong relationships that increase student cooperation and engagement. By looking beyond traditional approaches to behavior, we can help students become more skilled in regulation and problem solving. This book is for any educator who wants to help students reach better social, emotional, and academic outcomes.

—Julie Schmidt Hasson, EdD | Author, Keynote Speaker, Resilience Researcher

Compelling, deeply human, and actionable—The book every educator needs right now! Offering a 360° view of the challenges in today's schools, Stamper and Peck deliver science-backed strategies that can be put into practice immediately. Through no-judgment honesty and relatable stories, this book reveals what isn't working and provides a clear and innovative path forward. With its simple and effective framework, it equips educators to strengthen relationships, improve well-being, and cultivate thriving communities where everyone—kids, staff, and families—feels safe, supported, and empowered. Get ready to make real, lasting change happen.

—Lainie Rowell | Bestselling author, Award-winning educator, and International keynote speaker

For every educator who has struggled as they watched a student spiral out of reach, *The Language of Behavior* by Joshua Stamper and Charle Peck will become a go-to resource. With grace, wisdom, and practical solutions, this book peels back the layers of behavioral challenges to reveal a comforting and powerful truth; every action tells a story, and every story deserves to be heard. More than a guide, this is an opportunity to reimagine education as a collective effort built on empathy, curiosity, and understanding. It champions the vulnerable and reminds us of the resilient spirit in our students and our schools. Stamper and Peck offer strategies, and hope, as they remind us that no matter how lost we may feel facing these challenges, the heart of teaching lies in the connections we make. This is a must-read for anyone who believes in the transformative power of compassion in education.

—Kasey Schurtz | Instructional Facilitator, Podcaster

One of the biggest issues facing education today is behavior. Where do we even begin? I wish I had had access to *The Language of Behavior* when I was a classroom teacher and then a principal. The ideas and information from Joshua Stamper and Charle Peck are invaluable and necessary for anyone working with students. This book is a gamechanger and I will be passing it along to everyone I know.

—Todd Nesloney | Director of Culture and Strategic Leadership at TEPSA

The Language of Behavior is a game-changer for anyone working with students. Joshua Stamper and Charle Peck take what we often see as "misbehavior" and flip it on its head, showing us how behavior is really just a student's attempt at communication—a cry for connection, understanding, and support. Perhaps the most crucial component of the book is that Joshua and Charle don't just talk about the need for change; they give us the tools to make it happen. Their framework is simple, actionable, and full of heart, inviting us to create environments where trust and growth flourish. As they so powerfully put it, "Behavior is an expression of uncertainty, distrust, or instability, and addressing the underlying issue is the key to improving it." If you're ready to see your students—and yourself—in a whole new light, this book is for you.

—Brian T. Miller | Middle School Principal, Author, Speaker, and Podcaster

The Language of Behavior is a passion-driven, science-backed guide that will transform the way you understand, respond to, and address student behavior. Joshua Stamper and Charle Peck bring unparalleled expertise and a unique understanding to the challenges educators face daily, offering practical strategies grounded in empathy, science, and a commitment to being better for kids. This book empowers educators to move beyond punitive discipline, and toward building systems and supports that foster trust, connection, and growth. Through clear examples, guided thought exercises, and science-backed approaches to the conversation, Peck and Stamper provide a roadmap for creating supportive learning environments where every student feels seen, valued, and capable of achieving their potential. A must-read for teachers, administrators, and anyone dedicated to reaching all students, *The Language of Behavior* is a beacon of hope during a time when so many feel hopeless.

—Jeff Gargas | COO Co-Founder, Teach Better Team

In *The Language of Behavior*, Josh Stamper and Charle Peck challenge traditional approaches to misbehavior, urging us to reconsider how we interpret and respond to student actions. By addressing the impact of adverse childhood experiences and trauma, the authors provide a comprehensive framework through their three tenets: considering the environment, exploring behavioral breakdowns, and responding intentionally. This insightful book emphasizes the importance of collaboration among educators, caregivers, and communities to create supportive ecosystems for children. It is a must-read for anyone who fosters positive behavior change and regains trust in our educational systems. Transformative and actionable, it's a vital resource for educators today.

—Starr Sackstein | Author of *Student-Led Assessment, Hacking Assessment,* and *Making an Impact Outside the Classroom* and Consultant

In *The Language of Behavior: A Framework to Elevate Student Success,* Charle Peck and Joshua Stamper provide practical, actionable steps to reclaim the art of classroom management through approaches that are timely and appropriate for today's students and their families. Making the case for why traditional approaches no longer work, Peck and Stamper reset thinking from a paradigm of control to a more robust approach that empowers educators and students to constructively engage, address the real issues at play, and thrive both inside and outside the classroom. Providing real-world examples, the authors' voices ring true as authentic practitioners who have done the work and are now sharing what they've learned with educators everywhere. I heartily recommend this book to everyone working with students. It will transform your practice!

—Walter McKenzie | Educator, Mentor, and Founder of The Worthy Educator

As an educator deeply committed to rethinking traditional disciplinary approaches, I am thrilled to endorse *The Language of Behavior: A Framework to Elevate Student Success* by Joshua Stamper and Charle Peck. This book is a critical read for anyone seeking to transform the way we address challenging behaviors in schools. It's not only easy to read but packed with invaluable insights and actionable strategies that respect the complex backgrounds and needs of our students. Stamper and Peck expertly navigate the nuances of behavior through the lens of environmental influences, trauma, and mental health, emphasizing a compassionate, systemic approach to discipline that aligns perfectly with the Maslow Before Bloom philosophy. By prioritizing emotional and psychological safety, *The Language of Behavior* provides a blueprint for creating nurturing educational environments where all students can truly thrive. This book is a significant step towards a more empathetic, effective educational system.

—Dr. Bryan Pearlman, EdD | LMSW Founder & Head Trainer Most Valuable Professional Development

Joshua Stamper and Charle Peck's *The Language of Behavior: A Framework to Elevate Student Success* is a transformative and essential read for educators seeking to better understand and address student behavior. By replacing outdated punitive approaches with their three tenets—*Consider Your Environment, Explore the Breakdown, and Respond Intentionally*—the authors provide a clear, actionable framework to create supportive, trauma-informed learning environments. Filled with relatable anecdotes, research-backed strategies, and practical tools, this book challenges educators to see behavior as a language and respond with empathy and intentionality. Stamper and Peck empower teachers to not only guide students toward success but also foster trust, connection, and growth within their classrooms. *The Language of Behavior* is a must-read for educators ready to elevate their practice and make a lasting impact.

—Rae Hughart | Educator, Consultant, and Advocate for Transformative Teaching Practices

Many educators across our country understand that there is always a "why" behind positive and challenging behaviors displayed by our students...but struggle with access to a supply of strategies of what to do next. This book's relatable examples, relevant research, practical solutions, and concrete directions has an accurate pulse on what is happening in our schools today. As I read it, I find myself replaying and revisiting countless experiences we witness and live through daily. I am beyond excited to now have this resource in my back pocket!

—Andrea Bitner | EL Educator, Author, Speaker, Consultant

Table of Contents

Introduction: *Are We Failing?* 1
    Regaining Trust in the System 4
    Traditional Approaches to Misbehavior Aren't Working 5
    We're Misinterpreting Behavior 7
    A New Approach 8
    Purpose of the Book 9

Chapter 1: *Changing the Way We Respond to Behavior* 11
    Why Kids Aren't Behaving 11
    Adverse Childhood Experiences (ACEs) 12
    Trauma 14
    Mental Illness 15
    Struggling Caregivers 15
    Peer Conflict 17
    Escalation of Behavior 18
    Challenging Tradition 19
    Our Role in Behavior Prevention 20
    We're All in it Together 20
    Take Action 21

THE LANGUAGE OF BEHAVIOR

PART I: THE 3 TENETS OF BEHAVIOR

Chapter 2: *Tenet 1-Consider Your Environment* 25
    Background... 26
    Beyond Disengagement 28
    Empowerment from Within..................................... 29
    Tenet #1... 30
    Maintain Homeostasis.. 31
    Physical Space.. 32
    Social Space.. 36
    Integrating Strategies into Regular Practices 45
    Take Action.. 49

Chapter 3: *Tenet 2-Explore the Breakdown* 51
    Examining Student Behavior 54
    Identifying the Manifestations of Trauma in Behavior........ 57
    Recognizing Behavioral Signs and Symptoms of
        Trauma in Students... 63
    The Missing Puzzle Pieces 65
    Slow Build.. 67
    A Team Effort.. 68
    Implementing Tenet #2 69
    Take Action.. 71

Chapter 4: *Tenet 3-Respond Intentionally* 73
    Addressing Core Needs.. 75
    The Relationship Action Team................................. 76
    The First Strategies Implemented 79
    De-Escalation in Communication 87
    Avoiding Power Struggles.. 89
    Foundations of Behavior Change............................. 92
    Take Action.. 93

TABLE OF CONTENTS

PART II: THE ROAD AHEAD

Chapter 5: *Transforming Discipline Practices* 97
  In-School Suspension 97
  Keeping Students with the Content Expert 100
  Out-of-School Suspension 101
  Trust-Based Relational Intervention (TBRI) 104
  Discipline in the Classroom 106
  The Push-In Model for Minor Interactions 106
  Guiding Change: Three Steps to Shape Behavior 109
  Creating Personalized Behavior Action Plans 115
  Take Action 121

Chapter 6: *An Ecosystem of Support* 123
  Everyone is on the Team 124
  School Mental Health Audit 126
  Discipline Data as a Guiding Tool 127
  Gauging Progress 127
  Mapping Success with Monthly Results and Evolution 129
  Take Action 132

Chapter 7: *Addressing Setbacks* 133
  Team Check Ins 134
  Withstanding Changes 136
  Staff Turnover 136
  Budget Cuts and Resource Limitations 138
  Political and Social Climate 139
  Lack of Celebrating Successes 139
  Take Action 140

Chapter 8: *A Move Towards Change* 141
    Protective Factors..142
    Adaptability Across Settings............................143
    Educators..143
    Families...144
    Organizations..144
    Workplace..145
    Generational Change......................................146
    Take Action..147

References..149

Acknowledgments.......................................155

About the Authors.....................................157

More from ConnectEDD Publishing.......................159

INTRODUCTION

Are We Failing?

"Too often we forget that discipline really means to teach, not to punish. A disciple is a student, not a recipient of behavioral consequences."

–Dr. Daniel Siegel

Jacob, a 7th grade student, held his stomach as he walked down the hallway toward the nurse's office. Though he had permission from his teacher to leave the classroom, he forgot to grab a pass. Jacob has a reputation for extending his bathroom breaks and taking long strolls through the hall, so when his P.E. teacher, Mr. Johnson, notices Jacob, he stops him.

At this point, Mr. Johnson could respond in a few ways:

1. **Responding with Curiosity:** Mr. Johnson approaches Jacob calmly, asking, "Are you feeling alright? Where are you headed?" This approach prioritizes an understanding of Jacob's perspective before addressing the missing hall pass.
2. **Confrontation with Disorganization:** With a sharp, impatient tone, Mr. Johnson calls out, "Jacob, where's your hall pass?

I know you don't have one, do you?" Without giving Jacob a chance to respond, he continues, "You're always wandering the halls without permission." Mr. Johnson is abrupt and uses accusatory language, which immediately puts Jacob on the defensive. He doesn't attempt to verify the situation calmly or consider alternative possibilities, such as the reason for Jacob being in the hallway.

3. **Demanding with Authority:** Mr. Johnson reacts with intensity, moving in front of Jacob and stating, "Jacob, go back to class." Jacob, now irritated, tries to explain that he isn't feeling well and has permission to go to the nurse's office, but Mr. Johnson interrupts and says, "I don't want to hear any excuses. Get back to class." Visibly upset, Jacob tries to move past his teacher and says, "Get out of my way! I don't feel good." Mr. Johnson doesn't budge. Jacob, now angry, yells, "Move, or I will move you!" The principal hears the commotion from her office and intervenes. She motions for Jacob to go to her office and gets a quick rundown of what just happened from Mr. Johnson. He reports his version of events, emphasizing his belief that Jacob deserves to be punished for aggressive behavior and making a threat. Jacob gets sent to In-School Suspension (ISS) where he sits in frustration, discomfort, and isolation.

It's difficult to always know the intentions of all students. Teachers and administrators are doing their best to maintain order within a sometimes-chaotic system. What position might you have taken with Jacob? What might be the effects? We'll start by examining versions two and three.

In the second scenario, Mr. Johnson assumes Jacob is doing something wrong. Instead of asking him why he's in the hallway, his approach conveys distrust and lacks openness, while unnecessarily increasing tension. The interaction lacks structure, turning what could have been a simple inquiry into a confrontation.

In the third scenario, where Mr. Johnson takes an authoritarian stance, tension also rises. Jacob becomes guarded and reactive. As a result, he is punished with a trip to the ISS room. This is the least productive response because:

- **Jacob** felt unfairly treated. In his mind, he didn't do anything wrong, even though he did forget to obtain a pass from his teacher. When Mr. Johnson stepped in front of him and interrupted him, he felt backed into a corner and went into "fight or flight" mode. Ultimately, he didn't get what he needed and was left on his own without any guidance.
- **Mr. Johnson** was upset because Jacob was rude and noncompliant. He didn't believe the student received a harsh enough punishment. Now, Jacob is apprehensive about going to his P.E. class, and there is a disconnect between him and his teacher. He feels targeted and misunderstood.
- **The principal** was in a tough spot. She believed that Mr. Johnson was right to check for a hall pass but wondered if he could have handled it better. Jacob did have permission from his teacher but escalated the situation with Mr. Johnson. When he defied him and yelled, he crossed a line and needed to be reprimanded. ISS seemed like the only solution.

No one was left feeling satisfied or happy in versions two and three, and more animosity occurred. So where would you rather end up? We're thinking you'd rather be in a position to help Jacob become a trustworthy, successful student and get his needs met. We know educators have the best intentions and deeply care about kids, so responding calmly and with curiosity, the first option, is where we believe you'd rather be. This will lead to more effective outcomes where connection remains intact.

We are excited to share a simple framework in this book to help you navigate this and other common issues that pop up in our profession. We are optimistic about the future of education and know we can all work towards a more successful outcome *for everyone*, so let's get started!

Regaining Trust in the System

Mistrust occurs when we become reactive and use ineffective communication. Jacob could have had his needs met while receiving better guidance, and frustration could have been avoided altogether. Our goal is to instill trust within your school community. This is critical to student success and a thriving learning environment. Teachers need to feel supported when behavior issues arise, so how do we do that?

Well, first, we need to remember that regardless of a child's age, it is inevitable they will make poor choices at some point. So, we ask:

- Who is responsible for student behavior?
- Are typical consequences for misbehavior working to improve student behavior?
- How do we effectively mitigate chronic behaviors such as avoidance, aggression, and non-compliance?

When these questions go unanswered, we have confusion in the system and a cycle of mistrust. This compounds an already difficult process of working through student behavioral issues. However, when we accept that we're all responsible for guiding behavior and commit to navigating issues *with* students in a more supportive way, we will significantly improve the system. Below, we'll make an argument for why change is needed now and offer practical tools and strategies for you to use throughout the remainder of the book.

Traditional Approaches to Misbehavior Aren't Working

Over the years, Joshua, as an administrator, and Charle, as a former high school teacher turned clinical social worker, have seen relationships deteriorate and behavior intensify as school officials rely too heavily on punitive measures. When addressing student behavior, schools usually default to three forms of discipline:

1. Detentions
2. In-School Suspension (ISS)
3. Out-of-School Suspension (OSS)

Though these are becoming less common, in recent years, more than 2.5 million students attending U.S. public schools still received one or more out-of-school suspensions. Students who were assigned OSS missed a total of 11.2 million school days, with each student missing an average of 4.5 school days.[1] As a result, the following occurred:

Loss of Instructional Time: Similar to the data from the U.S. Department of Education Office for Civil Rights, in-school suspension (ISS) logs were filled with thousands of minutes lost by having students in the ISS room or sent home for OSS. Subsequently, teachers grew annoyed with having to get students caught up, and both parents and teachers were frustrated by their students' grades. There is an evident correlation between grades obtained and loss of instructional time with the content expert. Sitting in a room with an ISS clerk or "hanging out" at home is not a sufficient

---

[1] U.S. Department of Education Office for Civil Rights. (2021). An overview of exclusionary discipline practices in public schools for the 2017–18 school year [PowerPoint slides]. https://www2.ed.gov/about/ offices/list/ocr/docs/crdc-exclusionary-school-discipline.pdf

intervention to address the academic gaps created by removing students from the classroom learning environment.

Band Aid Fix: Suspending or removing a student may elevate or decompress the situation for the short term, but doesn't equip the student with essential skills to learn more appropriate behavior that may have resulted in a better outcome. If the student doesn't possess the skills to work through adverse or stressful situations, punishment will not magically create a skill set to help them better manage themselves through a fear-based approach. Sitting in isolation simply doesn't solve the underlying problem, nor will it prevent the behavior from occurring the same way in the future.

Lack of Restoration: By sending a student to ISS or to detention, we remove the ownership of fixing the destruction created by the student. Since every action has an outcome that impacts other people, the student may not realize how their behavior affected the person who felt violated. Instead, they may learn to avoid the person they bothered, opposed, or harmed and never learn to empathize or repair the relationship. Whether a student broke an object or fractured a relationship, the student needs to learn how to restore what was harmed. In a traditional ISS model, these skills are not modeled, taught, or implemented, which results in the student returning to an unresolved situation once the punishment is complete. Though we are making strides, we still lack proper staff training in this area.

Escalating Behaviors: We often place students in detention and ISS who have a difficult time sitting still and being quiet for long periods of time during the school day. Sending them to sit longer is counterproductive. In addition to this challenge, once they are sent to ISS or detention, students feel even more disconnected and generate negativity towards the school, the staff, and possibly other students who helped land them there. As a result, we may see escalated and poor behavior exhibited in detention or ISS, which leads to additional time assigned in these same settings. When students are placed back into their classrooms afterwards without guidance, skills, reflection, and a plan, it's no wonder these behaviors reoccur and may look even more hostile the next time.

We're Misinterpreting Behavior

In 2006, The New York Times shared an unfortunate story about a woman who wanted to celebrate love by having two Chinese characters tattooed on her left forearm with the translation "one love." Six months after having the tattoo, a store clerk saw the tattoo and informed the woman the characters meant something totally different. The Chinese characters on her arm actually meant "love hurts." Dismayed, the woman immediately consulted some of her bilingual co-workers about it. Each co-worker confirmed the tattoo was incorrect and translated to "love hurts." The woman immediately went and had the tattoo removed through a grueling laser process. This kind of misinterpretation is more common than we realize. The Chief Executive Officer (CEO) of Tattoo Removal Specialists in Beverly Hills, California, says his clinic has five or six new patients a week who discover their Chinese tattoos mean something drastically different from what they intended.[2]

Similar to the incorrect tattoo character experience, educators often misinterpret student behavior, focusing only on the surface-level actions without understanding the deeper meaning behind them. We may see a student behavior as deviant or disrespectful but with more investigation find a much deeper problem rooted in traumatic and dysfunctional experiences. Many students have difficulty understanding their emotions, regulating during stressful situations, and communicating their needs. As educators, it is our responsibility to acknowledge

---

[2] https://www.nytimes.com/2006/04/02/fashion/sundaystyles/cool-tat-too-bad-its-gibberish.html

that behavior is a language, and we must interpret students' actions to understand their emotions, experiences, and underlying needs so we can provide appropriate support for healing and growth. Our guidance and compassion are critical; our understanding and support, they may fall into despair and hopelessness.

A New Approach

In this book, we are providing an alternative way to respond to challenging behavior that is simple and effective. Our approach is based on three Tenets:

- Tenet 1: Consider Your Environment
- Tenet 2: Explore the Break Down
- Tenet 3: Respond Intentionally

Each of the 3 Tenets will be broken down and explained in later chapters. We'll also provide strategies to examine the nuances of interpreting behavior, assessing underlying issues, and devising creative solutions to foster a positive culture. These tenets will not only aid us in supporting youth as they navigate today's complex world, but they are also competencies to help our students build lifelong success, personally and professionally, well into adulthood.

Finally, we'll dive into how teaching behavior, creating opportunities to foster healthy relationships, and implementing alternative discipline practices can enhance students' readiness for the challenges and opportunities that await them. We'll demonstrate how to equip others with practical strategies to communicate more effectively and build lasting relationships. Ultimately, they will learn to:

- Reflect for Personal Growth
- Take Responsibility

- Feel and Be Empowered
- Advocate Effectively
- Restore and Regain Trust
- Create Personalized Action Plans

Purpose of the Book

Imagine a classroom where every student feels seen, understood, and valued. They engage willingly in the learning experience, ask questions, interact with their peers, and take risks as a means to grow and reach their full potential. It's not just an ideal; it's a reality we can form together.

The purpose of this book is to offer a new, simple approach to student behavior so we can improve common issues plaguing schools, families, and society. In the chapters ahead, we explore ways to:

- Improve well-being
- Increase retention rates
- Strengthen relationships
- Protect kids, staff, and families
- Reduce incidents of aggression
- Re-engage staff, students, and families
- De-escalate conflict more effectively
- Decrease frustration among all community partners

We are excited to take you on a journey that delves deeply into the profound effects of trauma and adversity on the lives of our students—which explains why much of their behaviors show up. In each chapter, we'll provide you with proven approaches empowering you to create learning environments that are not just inclusive, but genuinely supportive and safe.

We'll navigate this plan with a focus on fostering a sense of belonging for *everyone*. Through three simple tenets, we'll tap into the remarkable potential to nurture growth and healing in our fractured system and begin the process of accountability.

As we take you through a journey in the following chapters, we invite you to embrace the power of understanding, empathy, and proactive transformation. The pages ahead are packed with case studies, insight, actionable steps, and the potential to revolutionize the way we approach education. Together, we'll make a lasting difference in the lives of our youth, creating not just learners, but resilient, compassionate, and empowered individuals ready to embrace a world of amazing possibilities.

CHAPTER 1

Changing the Way We Respond to Behavior

"Every great dream begins with a dreamer. Always remember, you have within you the strength, the patience, and the passion to reach for the stars to change the world."

–Harriet Tubman

How do we get kids to behave better? This is the million-dollar question in education today. We're dealing with an entirely different generation of students who are moving through an outdated system, desperately communicating the need for change. If we want them to adapt, we must *listen* to their behavior and interpret it in clear language we can understand. Misbehavior tells us a powerful story. It's an expression of uncertainty, distrust, or instability, and addressing the underlying issue is the key to improving it.

Why Kids Aren't Behaving

Many students are walking around our buildings on edge, with an emotional charge in their nervous system, sometimes all day long. They generally lack skills, confidence, and self-awareness, so they avoid and react rather than advocating to get their needs met. Because they aren't coping while feeling incredibly uncomfortable and anxious, they become overwhelmed and "act out."

Children and teens have an inherent need for calm and comfort. When they feel nervous and aren't convinced they'll be OK, their emotions and negative thoughts fester and are eventually expressed behaviorally. Adults see their frustrating behavior as "bad" and want it to stop, so instead of helping them subsist, we tend to punish or isolate them, further perpetuating disconnect.

Below are common reasons for the emotional charge we mentioned above. With this foundational understanding, we can shift the way we think about behavior and provide the support kids and teens need to calm their nervous system.

Adverse Childhood Experiences (ACEs)

Adverse Childhood Experiences (ACEs) play a significant role in how many students engage in their learning environment. Consider this story about an avoidant 9th grade student, who we'll call Riley.

> Ms. Stein struggled to connect with Riley, a mild mannered, quiet student. She reported that Riley wore the same sweatshirt to school every day and avoided all group and partner work. Individually, Riley attempted his assignments but rarely completed them. It was a rocky start to high school for him, and Ms. Stein was concerned. She called Riley's mom who revealed that she and Riley were living in a women's shelter. They previously lived out of town but felt this was the safest place to land in an attempt to escape his abusive father. Riley's mom sounded defeated, though Ms. Stein could tell she was trying to do the best she could to protect her son. School was the furthest thing from Riley's mind, so just getting there to have some normalcy was the goal.

Kids like Riley who go unnoticed may sink into hopelessness after underperforming and disconnecting from school life. Since Ms. Stein cared enough to reach out to Riley's mother early on, she was able to connect him to resources. This intervention led him to engage more confidently with his peers and schoolwork.

Not all situations like Riley's are as pleasant. Sometimes kids get belligerent and aggressive like Jacob did in the last chapter when Mr. Johnson challenged him in the hallway. We try to shut down the behavior by exerting more power, or we "tiptoe" around them and get defensive. They might feel misunderstood or sense our rejection and internalize that they are "bad." They feel unlovable, and another blow to their spirit may make them spiral into despair.

In frustration, they think, why bother trying? The cycle goes something like this:

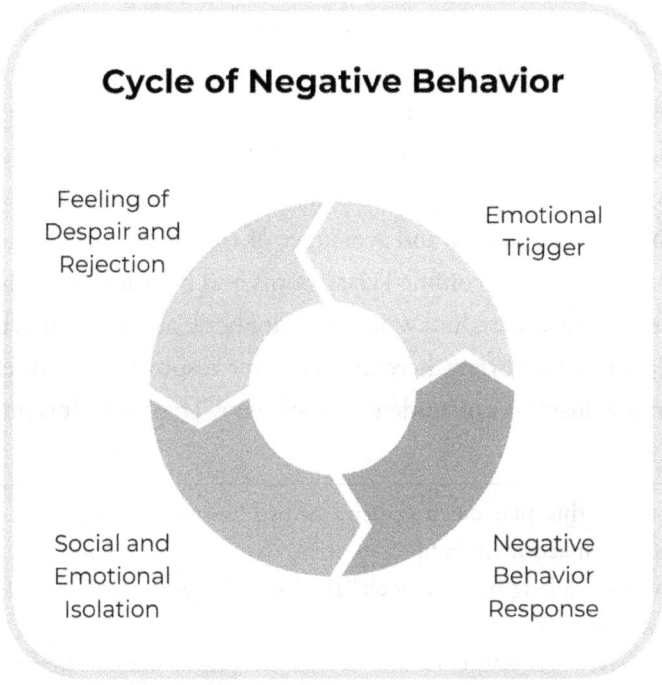

Rejection is a powerful emotion. Pushing others away is a tactic to avoid feeling the heavy weight of it. Young people trapped in this cycle develop poor self-worth and an "exaggerated fear" from which they feel they can't escape,[3] leading to behavior issues.

We, in turn, feel threatened with their subsequent disruptive behaviors and may enter the same physiological pattern of reactivity. Even when we try to hide our irritation and remain calm, our nervous system builds up an emotional charge, too. Ignoring it gives us a false sense of security though, in actuality, we're creating an unstable environment.

Trauma

Trauma is a potential outcome of an adverse childhood experience (ACE) and can have a dramatic impact on behavior. It can create a breakdown in the brain's neural pathways, and there's a strong link to all kinds of dysfunction in human behavior. Our body remembers trauma[4] but is often locked away subconsciously and can manifest initially as "exhaustion, confusion, sadness, anxiety, agitation, numbness, dissociation, confusion, physical arousal, and blunted affect" and later as "persistent fatigue, sleep disorders, nightmares, fear of recurrence, anxiety focused on flashbacks, depression, and avoidance of emotions."[5] No wonder kids are acting out in their confined classrooms and buildings that elicit constant uncertainty. We could write an entire book about trauma, but we'd like to just mention briefly here that a trauma response is definitely a culprit in many instances of student misbehavior. That's why it is important

---

[3] More on this phenomenon here: https://www.psychologytoday.com/us/basics/rejection-sensitivity?amp

[4] Discussed in length in the book "The Body Keeps the Score" by Bessel van der Kolk, MD (2014).

[5] Center for Substance Abuse Treatment (US). Trauma-Informed Care in Behavioral Health Services. Rockville (MD): Substance Abuse and Mental Health Services Administration (US); 2014.

to acknowledge the role trauma plays and seek to learn more about it as a part of our behavior response plan.

Mental Illness

This is another vast subject, so we'll just touch on the main points to demonstrate mental illness as an underlying cause for student behavior. According to the MTSS model, approximately 15% of students need Tier 2 intervention (e.g., small groups to target specific behaviors) and 5% need Tier 3 support to "individualize and intensify the intervention" using high quality evidenced-based practice, (e.g., individual therapy).[6] Though these interventions cover a wide variety of deficits—academically, socially, and emotionally—mental illness is often an underlying factor. Issues like anxiety, depression, self-harm, and suicidality are on the rise[7] which can cause great disruption for students. Those MTSS numbers above are pre-COVID, and many schools we work with are reporting higher numbers of issues since.

Acknowledging mental illness as a contributing factor to misbehavior removes shame and judgment. This happens when we accept that some behaviors are out of a student's control, at least at the onset, and can be improved with treatment. For example, if a student is tired, unmotivated, irritable, and frequently absent, they may suffer from depression. However, with medical and therapeutic support, they may be able to attend regularly and engage. Validating their symptoms and offering effective treatment will help them cope and function better.

Struggling Caregivers

Sometimes adults become threatening figures in the eyes of young people. We have our own ACEs and traumas to deal with. If we hold an

---

[6] Kentucky MTSS Implementation Guide, pg. 30
[7] Lancet Child Adolesc Health (2021); Bersia et al. (2022); McMahon (2023)

emotional charge all day long, we are at risk of developing health problems and may find it difficult to mask our instability. We may be the one to erupt or put up an emotional wall. We may decide to limit our time and energy at work or step out of the profession altogether. This creates more systemic instability for kids.

There are educators who are skilled and who make strong connections with kids even though they are battling their own adversities. Take, for example, this story from a seasoned teacher.

> I love teaching! By my 10th year in education, I was on top of my game. Around that time, however, I faced some personal challenges. My mother was diagnosed with Alzheimer's, and I lost my "sister friend" to cancer.
>
> I held it together most of the time but experienced weird incidents that crept up. I felt pain in my lower left leg and in my stomach, and my principal stopped me in the hall because I looked "sunken" and was concerned. I reassured her that I was doing fine, but I wasn't. In fact, I became easily irritable for things I could usually tolerate like chatty students during group work or interruptions over the PA. I found myself snapping at them more and engaging less, and student behavior issues in my class were on the rise. I realized I hadn't processed the stress and grief, and the way I was showing up to students wasn't working for them or me.

Without an awareness or understanding of the impact stress, trauma, and ACEs have on our nervous system, we will eventually find it difficult to function at our best. Since children feed off our energy, we need to keep our own mental health and well-being in check, too.

CHANGING THE WAY WE RESPOND TO BEHAVIOR

Peer Conflict

When we ignore behavior as a message or as a call for help, we miss opportunities. Consider this situation with a student named Ethan, a 9th grader who moved to New Jersey from Alabama and was relentlessly targeted for being different.

> Ethan was younger than most of his classmates, noticeably smaller, and quiet. Since he didn't have any friends, he often buried his head in a book and became an easy target for other kids to tease. Teachers didn't easily connect with him because he was guarded and bothered by the nuances of school life. Being socially awkward didn't help, and by the end of his junior year, he had endured countless derogatory comments, hallway nudges, locker pranks, and degrading social media posts. No one seemed to notice, and Ethan had difficulty advocating for himself. One day when one of the ringleaders cornered him and wouldn't leave him alone, Ethan lost it and screamed a threatening remark to get him to stop. It worked. The other student looked stunned and ran right to a teacher to report Ethan's comment (neglecting to share his own role in the exchange of course). Though the other student retreated, it wasn't the outcome Ethan was hoping for. He got a ten-day suspension and a harsh label on his record which eliminated him for an elite scholarship he was in line to receive.

This can be a devastating situation for kids. Since they lack advocacy skills, they may feel alone and isolated, and feelings of anger and frustration can build up. Impulsivity is common for kids without a fully developed prefrontal cortex, so they do rash things that can change the trajectory of their childhood if we don't take notice. Schools are doing a good job teaching students social skills, but we still see a flood of kids struggling with their peers, many of whom are still flying under the radar.

Escalation of Behavior

Maladaptive behaviors are already dysfunctional, so punitive measures further complicate the issue and create a great divide between students and educators. It leads to a buildup of frustration which contributes to non-conforming behavior, and the cycle continues. Kids like Ethan (above) and Jacob (in the introduction) become resentful and may follow a more destructive life path when no one sees them or believes in them. On the other hand, students who learn to fly under the radar while climbing the social ladder are celebrated and esteemed, even though their relentless behavior causes turmoil for others.

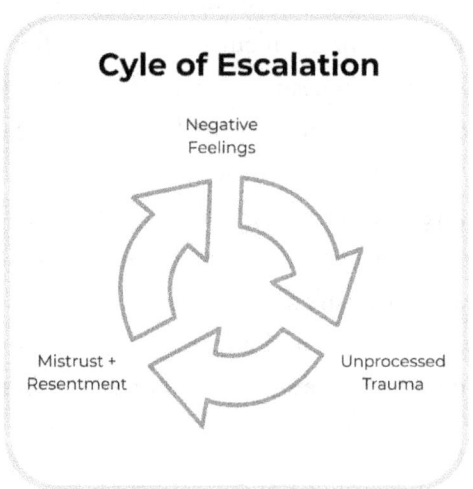

Sometimes we catch harmful behaviors in action and don't know what to do or feel so depleted that we simply ignore them. Other times, we don't know they're occurring at all and leave kids to fend for themselves. Historically, this is common practice. As we've mentioned, though, we have new norms. Young people experience life differently today than any other generation, so we need to shift our perspective, seeking to view the world through their lens in an effort to better support them.

Challenging Tradition

Our schools spend a great deal of time on traditional ways of responding to behaviors, such as punishment and sending kids away, and it's creating more issues:

- Reoccurrence
- Disengagement
- Disconnection
- Elopement (Escaping)
- Loss of instructional time
- A quick fix for deep-rooted issues

Some schools still permit corporal punishment, which creates more disruption to child learning; all organizations that aim to support child mental health, welfare, and future pathways are against this practice.[8] The mistrust we discussed in the Introduction of this book is the missing link, and the "you vs. me" mindset simply isn't working.

---

[8] "...the "American Academy of Pediatrics (AAP), the American Academy of Child and Adolescent Psychiatry (AACAP), the Society for Adolescent Medicine (SAM), the American Psychological Association (APA), and the National Association of School Psychologists (NASP). In addition, national education organizations including the National Education Association (NEA) and the American Federation of Teachers (AFT) oppose use of corporal punishment in schools, and the practice already is prohibited in all Head Start programs, schools managed by the U.S. Department of Defense (DOD), U.S. military training facilities, U.S. prisons and most juvenile detention facilities." (Kentucky Department of Education document, Kentucky Department of Education document, Trauma Informed Discipline Response and Behavior System, pg. 6)

Our Role in Behavior Prevention

Who is responsible for teaching children how to behave? The short answer: we *all* are. Let's think about our own practice since adults are the pivotal players in the transformation. Questions to ask yourself:

1. What am I doing that might be making student behaviors worse?
2. How might my beliefs about kids and their behavior create more conflict?
3. How am I experiencing behavior issues compared to my colleagues? Why is that?

Instead of becoming frustrated with seemingly "rude" students, we can channel that energy into solutions that fall within our control.

In the following chapters, we walk you through the 3 Tenets to help you successfully do this. We are also asking you to honestly assess where the struggle is really coming from. Sometimes, we need to consider how much frustration we are carrying within ourselves from past experiences or personal circumstances that may unfairly target kids. Just notice if you're one of the "struggling adults" we mentioned above and acknowledge that you may need extra support. If you're already functioning at your best, realize the power you have to influence change.

We're All in it Together

Teaching children how to behave cannot be the sole responsibility of parents and caregivers. Though parents should do most of the heavy lifting, we can't assume they have the capacity to do that all on their own. There is tremendous pressure to raise a child, especially in our fast-paced society, so it would be a relief and reward to the whole family system to use the "It Takes a Village" approach. We are responsible for student behaviors, too.

Take Action

Before we dive into the 3 Tenets framework in the next chapters, reflect upon your current practices. Think about **beliefs** you have about misbehavior. Some examples are:

- Kids shouldn't "get away" with misbehavior.
- Children need punishments and rewards.
- Every child is capable of growth and change.
- Misbehavior signals unmet needs or challenges.
- Punitive approaches can worsen underlying issues.
- Cultivating a supportive environment fosters positive behavior.
- Understanding and empathy are key in addressing misbehavior.

Think about the **approach** you use to address misbehavior. Some examples are:

- Punitive Measures: Reprimand behavior and enforce restitution.
- Handing Off: Send students to the office or to another adult.
- Isolation: Putting students in a space by themselves.
- Restorative Practices: Focus on repairing harm and promoting accountability.
- Positive Behavior Support: Use proactive strategies to reinforce positive behavior.
- Clear Expectations: Communicate and uphold clear rules for behavior.
- Individualized Support: Provide tailored interventions for each student's needs.

- Consistent Consequences: Apply fair consequences consistently for misbehavior.

Finally, honestly reflect on the following questions about your beliefs and approaches to student misbehavior:

1. How do my actions contribute to growing behavioral issues?
2. How do I influence the overall feel of the learning environment?
3. How does my response to misbehavior affect short- and long-term outcomes?

In the next three chapters, we outline a new framework (the "3 Tenets") that will simplify your behavior prevention and intervention plan, and in later chapters, we share collaborative approaches and tools to effectively measure outcomes.

PART I

The 3 Tenets of Behavior

CHAPTER 2

Tenet 1: Consider Your Environment

> *"Children are the products of an environment over which they have no real control—passengers through narrow pathways in a world they never made."*
>
> –Bryan Stevenson

The world we perceive is a mental construct, not necessarily reality. As individual beings, we possess a unique lens and experience our environment through our own senses, biases, histories, and cultural adaptations. Even when some of these are shared collectively, they never manifest exactly the same. When something occurs out of the norm, such as misbehavior, environmental influences merit closer examination. With careful consideration of how we set up the space we share with others, we can often prevent disruptions in the first place.

Sharing the burden of guiding behavior need not be arduous; rather, it's something we accept that is part of our role as educators at every age level. Schools share the responsibility of setting up a space to help kids learn and grow, though the traditional classroom is outdated and could better meet their needs.

We don't want teachers and support staff sending kids off to the school counselor to "deal with" them just like we want parents to avoid sending their kids to a therapist to "fix" them. That's not solving the problem and it's sending an unproductive message that "I can't handle you" or "I don't want you here." We might think we don't want that child with us, but it's really the behavior we want to disappear, not the child

Background

Imagine as a teacher spending hours planning and revising ideas into a well-crafted lesson during your limited down time at home. You're excited about sharing these fun learning activities with your students and can't wait to witness those "aha moments" you envision. In class, you take several minutes explaining, defining, and modeling the activity, and it's time for students to get into groups to work on their own.

"1-2-3-GO!" you announce. No movement, just chatter.

"OK, let's get into our groups and get started everyone!" Still nothing.

You scan the room only to see a complete disregard of your directive and a few blank stares as if to say, *huh?* Even when you restate the instructions, you hear sighs and whispered snide remarks. You feel your face get warm and your heart pound through your chest. Losing self-restraint, you blurt out in your best whiny voice, "Why did I waste my time doing this if you don't even care?!"

Now you've got their attention.

This is a frustrating part of teaching. Coming up with seemingly great ideas that flop or never gain the momentum we'd hoped for is disappointing at best. Even the most seasoned, captivating teachers have

TENET 1: CONSIDER YOUR ENVIRONMENT

experienced this. Leaders report similar issues when working with staff or parents. We mindfully play out a conversation in our mind prior to a meeting only to be taken off guard when the response is different than what we assumed.

> One day, Josh had a parent in the front office to see him. This was a parent who was very involved in their children's lives and someone Josh had multiple positive conversations with in the past.
>
> On this particular day, Josh asked the parent to come back to his office to discuss some important information about the student. Without any thought, Josh sat behind his desk and began to ask a variety of questions to get a better understanding of the situation.
>
> As the parent was talking, Josh noticed they were uncomfortable, which was very different from their previous interactions. The parent began to shift in their chair, fidget with their hands, and stumble over their words.
>
> Josh paused the conversation and asked, "Is everything OK?"
>
> The parent responded, "Mr. Stamper, I know I'm not in trouble, but it is very intimidating to be in the principal's office."
>
> This parent, like so many others, shared they had negative experiences in the school, specifically in the front office and with their childhood administrators.
>
> Josh immediately moved the meeting to the conference room and the parents body language and communication improved immensely.

Oftentimes, we perceive ourselves as the hero in the story solving problems and creating memorable outcomes for kids and families. When things don't go as planned, we wonder, *what went wrong?*

Beyond Disengagement

Many educators say they feel disenfranchised and find themselves constantly questioning whether it's worth it to stay in this profession. It's not what they signed up for. We discussed the underpinnings of this in Chapter 3 (remember processed trauma and an emotional charge?). Add continual challenging student behavior or frequent parent complaints to the mix, and we may completely derail.

Now, we'd like you to think more deeply about the overall scenario as we prepare you to put Tenet 1 into action. Let's first look at what educators across the country tell us about their experiences and see if you can relate. In training sessions, we often pose the question: *What are the top issues you have with students?* Typical answers are:

1. Avoidance
2. Non-compliance
3. Pushback
4. Aggression
5. Disrespectful talk
6. Chronic absenteeism

We then follow up with, "*What have you tried to mitigate these behaviors but isn't working?*" Typical responses include:

1. Call home
2. Talk with student privately
3. Office referral
4. Mental health referral
5. Ignore it
6. Call out students in front of peers
7. ISS (In School Suspension)
8. OSS (Out of School Suspension)

TENET 1: CONSIDER YOUR ENVIRONMENT

Others say they've tried *everything* but "nothing seems to work." Sound familiar?

So what do we do with non-compliance, apathy, and aggression? At this point, you might already be thinking that we need to consider the child's history and contemplate their behavior patterns (as discussed in Chapters 2 and 3). For example, why might the student be avoiding class? What happened to them to cause them to do this? These are great questions to ask, though we'd like you to include one more critical question: What *in this environment* may be contributing to this behavior?

Empowerment from Within

We need to embrace teaching not only academic content but also appropriate behavior. After all, behavior is an inherent part of whether academic standards will be mastered, so if we incorporate strategies to deliberately address it as a learning opportunity on all education levels, we evoke a new social norm.

We need to shift our assumptions that students will be compliant to assuming they *won't*. This isn't meant to be cynical; it's to be prepared. We can learn how to make better predictions about where their behavior is coming from so we can give them some grace and shift into problem-solving mode. We'll be ready, confident, and competent when misbehavior does arise, *because it will*, and less disappointed when they mess up.

Traditional education should be more supportive of leaders, too. Often, when administrators stray from the discipline matrix to use alternative and innovative strategies, the tendency is to question and criticize the new practice without assessing the result of the practice. Leaders are charged with being creative when it comes to implementing assessment, grading, and teaching practices. However, leaders are often chastised by the district, teachers, and/or parents for incorporating new behavior practices with our students. Tenet #1 shows us what to do as individuals within the system so we don't age out while desperately waiting for change.

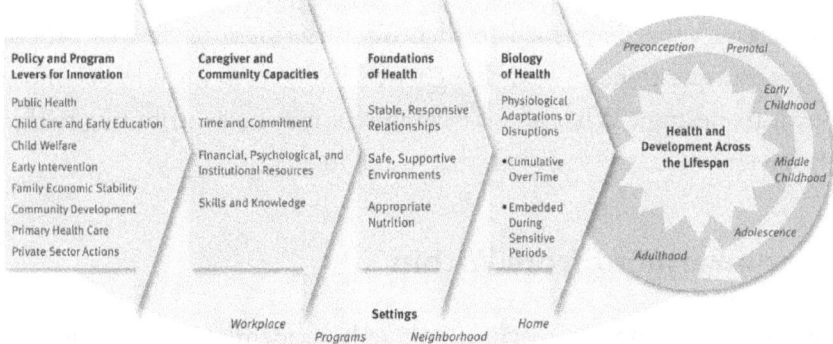

National Scientific Council on the Developing Child and the National Forum on Early Childhood Policy and Programs from Harvard University

Tenet #1

The first tenet in our framework is *Consider Your Environment*. When implementing this tenet consistently, we instill security and prevent behaviors from occurring so frequently in the first place. Maladaptive behavior always tells a story and can help us identify what's contributing to it or missing from it. Typically, it starts with feeling unsettled or insecure in our surroundings where our sense of safety appears compromised. Nurturing security and stability is the best approach in a behavior prevention plan. We control a significant amount of what goes on in our classroom or office.

But any framework for improving the status quo must be simple, or we won't do it and will lose hope all over again. Setting up a new environment can feel overwhelming, so we're making this easy. Tenet

TENET 1: CONSIDER YOUR ENVIRONMENT

#1 simply requires that you *consider*, not *overhaul*, your current environment, which we break down below.

Maintain Homeostasis

The environments we spend time in can have lasting effects. When our nervous system is on high alert, it impacts our physical health and even produces inflammation.[9] If this occurs frequently, it negatively impacts our health and wellness, preventing us from functioning at our best and resulting in long-term implications. It's difficult to respond effectively to the needs of others when we're overcharged, and since we are taking on the responsibility to help raise our youth collectively, we all need to feel energized and alert more consistently.

Our lives are better when we feel excited and comfortable within our jobs and relationships, so having a plan to get ourselves back to baseline when something does charge us, creating a resting, calm nervous system is imperative. Staying in that state of homeostasis takes practice and a willingness to try.

> Angelina, a high school special education teacher, puts a raspberry scratch-n-sniff sticker in her pocket. When she feels overwhelmed, she pulls the sticker out, brings it up close to her face, and draws in the scent which places her back in her grandmother's vast field of raspberry plants. She spent time with her siblings here in her youth, and the memory brings her immediate joy. In turn, she feels calm and stays regulated. Because this small act prevents the flood of stress hormones through her nervous system, she responds to challenging student behavior with ease and patience.

---

[9] Hairston, Stephanie. (2019, July 11).

It may seem silly to "think of your happy place" like Angelina did. However, if it has a powerful effect on our senses and can actually prevent overwhelming stress, why not include it in the plan? There are other ways to take us back to a place of serenity such as drawing a picture and hanging it in the room at eye level, putting a motivating quote on the bulletin board, or thinking of a song. Having a plan that is most relevant to our own experiences is the best approach. The goal is to create a harmonious, peaceful space that can adapt to the ebbs and flows of the day. We examine ways to create an environment of calm below.

Physical Space

Have you ever wondered what students think or feel when they enter a new space? Maybe it's a classroom, office, hallway, bus, or cafeteria. As new teachers, one of the first things many of us envision is what our classroom will look like:

- What will be the overall theme?
- How will desks be organized?
- Where will the rules be posted?
- Where would be a good place to post student work?
- How will I design my award-winning bulletin board?

It's an exciting time! Those are important questions to ask. Just as we need to make sure our classroom is conducive to a productive learning experience, it's equally important to consider how our space might *be experienced*. When setting up a space for students ask:

- What might their first impression be?
- How will they feel to be here?
- Am I meeting their needs beyond mine?

TENET 1: CONSIDER YOUR ENVIRONMENT

If we're setting up our office, we could ask the same questions regarding a parent or staff member:

- What might their first impression be?
- How will they feel to be here?
- Am I meeting their needs beyond mine?

In fact, we could ask these questions at home, in a corporate office, or in any staff room. These simple questions could make a major difference because we step outside of ourselves to consider others, and when issues do arise, we can go back to thinking about the way they might be experiencing our shared space.

> Jessa was a highly intelligent, gifted child who was reading by the age of 18 months old and with fluency by age 2. While reading a district bulletin, she saw a summer Spanish class advertised and asked her parents to enroll her because she wanted to learn a new language. Her parents were thrilled and decided to set Jessa up by enrolling her in a French Immersion school at the start of 1st grade. As her parents watched her tiny frame board the bus for a forty-five-minute ride to this elite school, they wondered if they made the right choice. After a few weeks, Jessa's teacher, Madam Bouchard, called home.
>
> "I had to move Jessa to the back of the room near me because she is bothering other kids." Apparently Jessa was humming while doing her work and other kids were frustrated with her. Jessa's parents spoke with her at school, and she agreed to stop humming.
>
> A week later, Madam Bouchard called again.
>
> "Jessa is so disorganized. Her desk is a mess, and she has a lot of random pieces of paper with drawings stuffed in there."

Again, Jessa's parents spoke with her at home and Jessa agreed to stop drawing and be more organized.

When an alarming call came in from Jessa's teacher again who reported that Jessa was found in the stairwell with her arms around her knees rocking, it was time for a meeting.

Upon entering the classroom, Jessa's parents noticed the walls were filled with many different colorful posters and motivational quotes. There were blinking mini lights stretched around the bulletin board and desks were closely lined up next to each other with barely any space to move freely. They sat down at the small table at the back of the room listening to Madam Bouchard's concerns.

"I'm cautious about saying this, but Jessa has signs of autism."

"Autism?" Jessa's mom asked.

"Yes, I'm hesitating to say that but it's what I think. Jessa is acting out a lot in class, and her behavior looks like other kids I've had with autism."

Jessa's parents pulled her from the French Immersion school and placed her back at the school just down the street in her neighborhood. After just a week, Jessa's new 1st grade teacher reported that she was happily engaging in classroom activities and was behaving "normally." Jessa was not autistic. She was overstimulated. In this new environment, she was thriving.

Instead of labeling Jessa, her teacher could have considered the behaviors Jessa displayed as an expression of extreme discomfort. Without asking questions and making unfair judgements, we're missing important connections we could be making and, in fact, contributing to the disruption.

TENET 1: CONSIDER YOUR ENVIRONMENT

Include Senses Everything we do influences our brain chemistry, whether it is a positive or negative experience. The physical space can have an immediate influence on us through our senses, and because each individual has a unique life experience and genetic disposition, no one person will have exactly the same experience as described in the introduction of this chapter. If we ignore the way kids react, we might contribute to their misbehavior like in Jessa's story.

Conversely, our physical space can contribute to a sense of security. Some kids (and adults) need to know how to easily exit the classroom if there's an emergency or urgency to use the bathroom. Others need a quiet place to escape to when there is a lot of movement or when the noise gets overwhelming. A tent with blankets, pillows, and books can work miracles, while others might respond positively to looking down at a puzzle right at their desk.

Considering the individual needs of each child who spends ongoing time in your space can make a difference between a moment of disruption and full-blown meltdown.

Remember ACEs Some children are more disadvantaged than others with a more chaotic or unsettled nervous system, and educators and school mental health staff would benefit from being better equipped to establish a more secure environment for them. Specific training on how childhood trauma shows up behaviorally and how attachment disruption affects the types of behaviors that are in our control (and not) would have a positive impact on the way our children are educated.[10] Still, without extensive knowledge, the basic information we provide in Chapter 2 is enough to warrant analysis and action on what we're currently doing and a commitment to making adjustments that will best suit our students' needs.

---

[10] O'Neill et al. (2010).

Social Space

The goal in setting up a secure social space is coherence. Imagine having a learning environment that intentionally and consistently seeks interconnectedness and an understanding of each other's needs. Not in a way that will elicit eye rolls like playing icebreaker games. Rather, attuning to one another's mood and disposition with a genuine care and regard for them as a human being.

Now let's think about *incoherence.* This creates disconnection where people within the system work in silos or feel left out of the larger group.[11] What message might this send? It is, at best, confusing. It creates disconnect (to classmates, staff members, leadership team, school community, etc.), which lands us in an internal and external conflict about who we are and where we belong. In adolescence, this is closely tied with the formation of identity and can have a long-term negative impact on our self-worth. If we feel like an outsider, we wonder if others perceive us as unworthy, even when we're being told, "You matter."

Think about what occurs in the teaching profession. We hear, "You are valued," and "Practice self-care," though educators certainly don't buy into this when more work and responsibilities are piled on without proper time or training. This goes beyond confusion—it creates distrust.

Now think about how kids internalize messages about growth mindset. The "reach for the stars" and "you can do anything you put your mind to" attitude is thwarted as soon as they get a mediocre test score since these numbers are what are truly valued and celebrated in our current system.

---

[11] A report funded by the Bill & Melinda Gates Foundation and published by the RAND Corporation explained incoherence in relation to an instructional system as occurring "when one or more components are not linked to other messages within the larger instructional system or provide conflicting signals…" (Pauketat et al., 2023)

TENET 1: CONSIDER YOUR ENVIRONMENT

Tangible ways to consider our social environment to create a culture of coherence and connection are suggested below:

The Relationship Inventory During administrative walkthroughs, Joshua and his administrative staff noticed discrepancies between teachers' intentions and their actions. Each teacher on campus expressed how important it was to build a solid relationship with their students and the benefits of engaging with each student throughout the duration of class. However, during the busyness of the passing period and during class, teachers would participate in other tasks, such as checking their email, organizing their supplies, or grading student work. The Relationship Inventory was constructed as a simple checklist to assess and reflect on how often they are actively completing the most important and impactful practices each day:

- Do you consistently greet students at the door as they enter the classroom to create a welcoming environment?
- When communicating with your students, do you make an effort to smile, conveying warmth and positivity?
- Do you regularly say, "Good Morning" or "Good Afternoon" to acknowledge and engage with your students?
- Are you intentional about asking low-level questions to better understand your students beyond the subject matter?
- Do you actively listen and give full attention when your students communicate with you?
- Are you mindful of pronouncing and using your students' names correctly to show respect and value for their identity?
- Do you make an effort to say something kind or offer words of encouragement to your students?
- Do you provide physical gestures of affirmation such as hugs, high fives, or handshakes to build rapport and connection?
- Do you create opportunities for students to collaborate and work as a team, fostering a sense of community and belonging?

- Are you proactive in offering tangible options and choices to empower your students in decision-making and problem-solving?
- Do you make time for one-on-one conversations with your students to build individual connections and understand their unique needs?
- Are you approachable and open to students approaching you with questions, concerns, or simply to chat?
- Do you show empathy and understanding towards your students' challenges and struggles?
- Are you consistent in providing positive reinforcement and recognition for your students' efforts and achievements?
- Do you actively seek feedback from your students to understand their perspective and improve your teaching practices?
- Are you transparent and honest with your students, fostering trust and authenticity in your interactions?
- Do you celebrate diversity and inclusivity in your classroom, recognizing and respecting each student's background and experiences?
- Are you willing to apologize and admit mistakes when necessary, modeling humility and accountability for your students?
- Do you encourage student autonomy and independence while still providing necessary support and guidance?
- Are you mindful of your non-verbal cues and body language, ensuring they align with your words and convey respect and care for your students?

For leaders, the most important aspect of the Relationship Inventory is to use the checklist, in partnership with the teacher, as a reflection of best practices, not an indictment of the learning environment. If utilized with non-judgmental support, the inventory can be a powerful

TENET 1: CONSIDER YOUR ENVIRONMENT

reminder that positively impacts student relationships and promotes a safe environment.

Consistency Consistency breeds predictability. Predictability provides security. As soon as we receive conflicting messages, we form narratives that draw upon our personal histories. While we sit with those unresolved stories, they ruminate in our daily thoughts and invade typical, healthy thinking patterns. Imagine the downward spiral a developing child with lagging skills might get sucked into.[12] Many of them get stuck there. And others simply get ignored. When we don't notice, we do a tremendous disservice to kids.

We all make up our own stories in the midst of incongruence or conflict. Worse, we might tell ourselves stories that are biased or untrue. We may withdraw or disregard norms or guidance if we don't trust that the leader is looking out for us and, instead, prefers others in the group. We create even more uncertainty and insecurity, which is the opposite of what we want for our kids, especially those who are struggling to manage the ACEs and trauma as described in Chapter 2. We go into protective mode (remember the amygdala), and without consciously trying to resolve our issues, we risk building up anger and resentment. That "disruptive behavior" is a manifestation of frustration. It looks like avoidance, backtalk, and attitude and all those "behavior issues" we listed earlier in this chapter. With a willingness to consider our environment and how others may experience it, especially children and adolescence, we position ourselves toward more equitable practices to benefit students academically and personally. Misbehavior shows up less frequently when we consistently try to meet—or at least validate—everyone's needs.

Acceptance The power of acceptance goes a long way in building positive relationships with others. Accepting someone's choices,

---

[12] Dr. Ross Green (2024) shares his research and insight on how lagging skills creates frustration and leads to misbehavior. He also https://www.additudemag.com/lagging-skills-unsolved-problems-alsup/

appearance, and beliefs does not mean we have to acquire them ourselves. Instead, it sends the message that "you *are* valued," even when we disagree. Emotionally intelligent people can step outside of themselves and still honor someone across from them as a human being. It does not mean we need to allow them to mistreat us; it simply means we relinquish control over them. We're essentially saying, "I can separate your choices from mine, but I will still treat you with dignity."

Consider their intention. Behaviors don't always match true intention, especially among children, because they're still learning how to effectively communicate. Kids want to perform well. They want to be liked. They want to be appreciated. When we accept others for who they are in the moment and realize they have their own unique history and challenges, we foster trust. We need to let go of our desire to change people's minds. It creates conflict and can be exhausting. Most importantly, it puts up a barrier that may damage or sever the relationship altogether and that can have detrimental effects such as eliciting more disruptive behavior issues and absenteeism.

When we use these simple approaches, others won't feel as if they're cornered and will therefore feel less threatened. Their stress system will be in more of a steady state and less reactive. Disruptive behaviors are less likely to occur, and the environment remains more stabilized.

Courtesy All children are humans and, as such, are deserving of kindness and courtesy. In fact, all people deserve this at a basic human level. If we are not regarded with civility, we are at risk of forming a deep frustration and mistrust of others and may constantly question the intention of others.

Leaders earn respect when they listen and are cordial rather than imposing their status and authority. Sometimes we forget how powerful the simple notion of politeness and respect for others can be, so this is a simple reminder to set up the social space with the same virtue. For example, when approaching a student while they're talking to a friend, say, "Sorry to interrupt your conversation," or "Excuse me for a sec," or some other nicety. Imagine how that feels to give this respect to someone in a subordinate position.

Keeping instructions short and clear is another way to extend courtesy. Time is incredibly valuable to *everyone*, so fewer words are better. As soon as we notice someone understanding our point, we can stop talking and move on rather than overextend the message. We also can avoid talking *at* people and consider the effect our conversational style has on them.

Presence What do you think about when you hear "close talker"? Maybe it's the Seinfeld episode, or maybe you cringe because you recall someone who invades your space, and you plot your escape route as they approach. When observing classrooms, we sometimes notice the space between student and teacher is invaded. This practice can shut kids down, especially adolescents. This stage in particular can be awkward, and they're more conscientious and protective of their body and space. Their amygdala goes on alert when adults get too close, and we need to be fully aware of our own positioning while around them. Are we standing too close? Are we loud? Do we smell weird to them? Is our tone negative or judgmental?

People become annoyed for a variety of reasons. In Cincinnati, Ohio, a local radio show, *Jeff & Jenn on Q102*, do a segment called, "The Second Date Update." People call in who have been "ghosted," or ignored, after a first date and the caller asks the host to call them on their behalf. There are a number of reasons why people feel incompatible after just one meeting, and they range from typical to downright outrageous. Take one person who ignored the caller because their apartment decor was full of "cheap" looking furniture which was the turn off. What they didn't know was that the caller was actually loaded but lived modestly. They made a character assumption based on a quick scan of the environment and missed an opportunity for a potential connection.

Sometimes people are holding on to something we did from an earlier time that hasn't been resolved. Maybe it has nothing to do with us at all. Perhaps something subconsciously is festering, and we happen to be the one who sparks it unintentionally or unknowingly. Still, common courtesy helps to cushion this which can influence the level of escalation when a problem does arise and it's easier to maintain connection when something does go wrong if we stick to this ethic.

Approachability How many times do we judge people just by looking at them? Our brain takes shortcuts by making assumptions, and whatever merit our assumptions have won't matter if we've already made a decision based on them. For example, if a student needs extra help with their report but has formed the opinion that their teacher "seems mean," they might avoid them and miss out on learning, improving their grade, or a potential connection. The real disappointment is that the student may have adopted this belief based on a single interaction or rumor alone.

When working with kids, it's especially important to set up a space of safety and security and consider how we appear to them. When we aren't intentional about this and neglect to build rapport, we miss the opportunity to establish trust. We know that when kids feel unsafe or uncertain, they may act out, avoid, or disengage altogether. This isn't what we want in our schools or workplace.

TENET 1: CONSIDER YOUR ENVIRONMENT

> A seasoned hospital-based therapist we coached, Miguel, told us about the time he was appointed to run a teen therapeutic group and felt like there wasn't much progress. He wanted to abandon the role and go back to providing 1:1 support where he thrived, but that wasn't an option, and a new group would be starting soon. After some discussion and careful reflection, he told us that a patient told him he had an RBF ("resting bitch face"), and couldn't get past it. Leading a therapy group made him feel like a failure. There was a disconnect with the teens because he felt like he needed to put up a stronger front. In the group setting, he wanted to assert more authority to keep them all safe and on task to align with the therapy goals. Miguel shifted his approach. He made deliberate attempts to soften his disposition (posture, facial expression, tone, etc.) and became flexible with discussions. When checking in a few weeks later, Miguel reported that the group climate was positive and the teens were responding well.

Being approachable means we're giving off a signal that the risk is low to seek us out and therefore, we elicit more attempts at connection. Because Miguel made a simple, but important, adjustment to his demeanor, he appeared less threatening.

Many studies report substantial benefits of connection on performance and wellness[13] so it is critical to get this right. Transforming the education space to equally value everyone: students, staff, support staff, parents/caregivers, volunteers, etc. will have positive outcomes everywhere, and having a socially coherent classroom, building, culture and climate benefits kids and their families.

Distractions What is the most significant distraction in the classroom today? We suspect it's a clear consensus that cell phones, and all

---

[13] CASEL, KAPPAN

their applications, are top of mind. There are plenty of reasons to ban cell phone use in the classroom, though some will argue that teaching kids how to use cell phones responsibly is needed or that a Zero Tolerance policy is impossible to regulate which just causes more conflict.

There is concern that youth (and adults) have an unhealthy reliance on their phones and that there is an interference with learning and social engagement with a cell phone in reach.[14] Some scholars, such as Dr. Jonathan Haidt (2023), say that issues underlying youth mental health have a direct link to the emergence of smartphones and social media and should be more regulated.[15]

Other evidence shows that zero tolerance policies don't actually improve school climate or curb student behavior.[16] We're not here to defend either approach because each community and culture varies and with time, other issues with these devices will undoubtedly emerge. However, since we are concerned about the developing child and aim to prevent and respond more effectively to behaviors, it's important to point out this controversial issue as a part of the implementation plan and consideration of environmental influences.

Sharing data and a rationale with students, staff, and caregivers when making decisions about how issues like this are handled is crucial. We often think that writing a policy with a brief explanation in the handbook will cover it, but when we make a change in the environment, we gain more buy-in when we share stories, statistics, expert perspectives, and direct impact on wellness with open discussion, or at least an explanation. We also build trust by communicating in a variety of ways that decisions are made to ultimately support developmental and health needs.

---

[14] Tanil & Yong (2020)

[15] https://www.afterbabel.com/p/phone-free-schools?r=182klo&utm_campaign=post&utm_medium=email

[16] American Psychological Association Zero Tolerance Task Force. (2008).

Check Yourself Though many adults appear to be functioning well, they may be compartmentalizing too much. It's OK to put on your "game face" or "fake it 'til you make it." Over time, however, this avoidance may make those raw, painful feelings eventually erupt or implode which disrupts the secure space we're trying to establish or stabilize for others, namely kids.

When we're carrying around guilt, shame, and pain that hasn't been processed, we are more susceptible to becoming emotionally charged. How many of us are walking around like this, and how can we secure a space for others when we're operating this way?

Others, especially kids, sense a change in our energy, so it's important to keep that in check. The best way to do this is to monitor our own body responses to stress. When we notice a shift in our mood or physiology, we can pay closer attention to what we need to remain calm. Moving from comfort to discomfort or contentment to irritability, for example, may spark an emotional charge which will cause increased heart rate, flush face, clenched jaw, nausea, etc. That's when we can ask ourselves, "What do I need?"

It's also OK to wonder if we're seeking control. In fact, we already mentioned this is a contributing factor to chaos when introducing Tenet #1. The problem is, trying to control people and situations creates a colossal barrier to connection and breaks down trust. Fast. If we're completely honest with ourselves, we can identify our need for constant order and find ways to stop chasing it. Once we understand *why* we have such a strong desire for it, we can shift into a new way of thinking that builds bridges and deconstructs barriers.

Integrate Strategies into Regular Practice

The space we're creating for others may be distracting or overwhelming as earlier discussed. When properly skilled and confident with varied strategies that integrate into daily practice, we prevent conflict and escalation. This is not something we have to plan. We simply have an awareness of our own behavioral patterns and those of others, we can shift gears more readily as a means to shift the experience in the environment. When we build meaningful relationships with those we regularly share space with, we learn to attune to their shifts in affect, attitudes, language, tone, etc. which alerts us to deploy a strategy.

Consider an athlete who plays their sport in an area with defined dimensions, such as a basketball, volleyball, or tennis court. After years of experience, they are well-practiced at anticipating whether a ball will be out of bounds as it moves towards them. We need this astute awareness of our students' shifts, too.

Adults need to learn more about our own brain/body connection to build this self-awareness in order to be most effective. Furthermore, since the other part of the equation is to respond to the needs of others, we also would benefit from learning about the developing brain as various stages of the lifespace influence behavior patterns.

Finally, we typically seek therapeutic support only when we've "hit rock bottom" or reach a point of utter frustration, but what would happen if these tools and skills were built into instruction?

Don't Push or Pull We can't push someone into feeling safe and we can't pull them into it either. They may not or cannot receive or accept that, so setting up a space that is consistently secure will prevent issues from occurring in the first place or will make it easier for them to come back to baseline when they do go offline. We want their nervous system to come to a rest when heightened or emotionally charged so if we keep this in mind, it will help.

TENET 1: CONSIDER YOUR ENVIRONMENT

> Practice: What can you say to yourself that will help YOU reframe the behavior so YOU don't go offline? We need to shift from protection mode to connection mode so what will help you do that? This is your go-to phrase to say out loud or to yourself the next time a student does _____.

Transition Time Ironically, students who hold their outbursts only for certain adults may mean they actually trust those adults more than anyone. Children who trust this caregiver know they will be loved even after an expression of overstimulation or emotional pain and will elicit judgment, isolation, and rejection elsewhere. Their environment may have unforeseeable triggers that conjure unbearable memories and can emotionally charge the child. When this occurs, children need love, acceptance, and validation more than ever, though that is challenging for an adult who does not understand why the child is misbehaving. We get charged and irritated and want to avoid these circumstances, but the role of the caring adult is essential to restoring trust. Kardiner and Spiegel (1947) demonstrated this between combat soldiers and their leaders. Early on, this relational connection was recognized as being crucial in the treatment of psychological breakdowns as well as in their prevention. Thus, one of the earliest approaches to treating combat soldiers was to get them back to the front line and back with their fellow soldiers and leader as quickly as possible after a physical or emotional injury. The tenets of frontline psychiatry led to more research on the protective factors of morale, group cohesion, leadership, and training (van der Kolk, 2007)."

Changing Rooms When we master these practices, kids may express an unmet need or their frustration more frequently *because* they feel safe here. They may want to be in this space rather than anywhere else, so if there is a threat to move environments, such as a bell ring, they may become disruptive. Or, if they don't want to be elsewhere, they may misbehave as a means to get back into this space. This is maladaptive, though it is a pattern we need to pay close attention to; it means there is a perceived threat that needs to be explored. It's good practice to assess if there is a relationship disconnect or a potentially harmful situation prompting them to react. Ideally, all kids will want to share space with everyone, everywhere in the building.

Down Time What is there to do when students finish with their work? How do they come in to start the class? What do they do with the 2-3 minutes while anticipating the bell? Preparing for these lag times can make a significant impact on the way students engage in a group setting. Consider how these times will be filled so that all the energy we've put into creating a safe and secure environment remains that way. Tenet # 1 focuses on setting up the environment to promote and maintain safety, security, and stability with a space engaging harmoniously *together*.[17]

Peer Engagement Providing children with opportunities for peer interaction typically helps prevent behavior issues and fosters an atmosphere of support.[18] More instances of peer influence can reduce the power imbalance of the "traditional teacher vs. students" dynamic in the classroom setting, so it's sound practice. Ultimately, integrating peer engagement throughout the day, such as partner work or play, can be valuable and promote healthy growth and development.

---

[17] HeartMath Institute Research Staff (2016)

[18] "Intergroup Contact Theory (Allport, 1954; Pettigrew, Tropp, Wagner, & Christ, 2011), wherein providing individuals with opportunities for positive, cooperative, and supportive interactions can enhance attitudes, interactions, understanding, and support of others. Such positive interactions provide the opportunity to learn about and build relationships with others." (Valiente et al. 2020)

TENET 1: CONSIDER YOUR ENVIRONMENT

Take Action

Consider the experience of all students and adults who share the space and determine adjustments you can make that might prevent dysregulation and conflict, for them *and* you.

- **Start With Strengths:** We're all doing *something* right. In fact, we know most educators already establish great rapport with students and have already been considerate of seating arrangements and routine procedures. List the strategies and practices you are currently doing to create harmony in the space.
- **Physical Space:** Consider your physical space including sensory supports or distractions.
- **Social Space:** Where can students sit who may have been negatively targeted by a classmate? Who might you place a new student next to?
- **Your Space:** List all the ways the space supports your needs and anything you'd like to acquire to make that even better.
- **Transitions:** List all the transitions you anticipate and match 2-3 strategies you can incorporate to help these go smoothly.
- **Bathroom Breaks:** Consider what you'll do when students need to use the bathroom. What about when you need to use the bathroom? Think about the path and procedure students (or others) will use to do this.
- **Other Breaks:** Consider what you will when you notice the energy level is too high or too low. We suggest not trying to "power through" lessons, meetings, or presentations when you notice your audience isn't engaged. We recommend Rapid Resets (Peck & Caswell, 2023) for a quick shift in energy or when laughing or movement will benefit kids (and you). You may also notice the room is overstimulated (too loud, unstable). Implementing a Rapid Reset, music, turning off the lights, or

a short meditation video can help. Have an inventory of these within reach so you don't have to scramble to find it when you need it.

- **Other Adults:** Identify the skills and abilities of other supportive adults within reach. Maybe you have a fun and lively paraeducator who can break into song or a co-teacher who is incredibly patient and can tap in.
- **Calming Tools:** Create an inventory of strategies that work well to keep you clear-headed and integrate it into your everyday practice to prevent overwhelm.
- **Protective Check-Ins:** Consider the history (distant or recent) as a preventative approach to behavior to ensure the student (or staff member) is seen, heard, and valued. Establishing consistent time to build trusting relationships with students is crucial for gaining insight into their thoughts, feelings, and experiences. When students feel safe, comfortable, and supported, they are more likely to open up about their current challenges, emotions, and behaviors. Use these check-in opportunities to build rapport, address concerns, and offer guidance and support.

CHAPTER 3

Tenet 2: Explore the Breakdown

"Setting goals is easy; achieving them is hard."
–Elliot T. Berkman

> One afternoon, I received a call on the radio that a teacher needed assistance in her classroom. I was in my office meeting with my mentee, a coach who was getting his Masters in Educational Administration, and I told him to come with me to gain additional experience.
>
> When we arrived, the teacher was standing outside her door monitoring her class and keeping an eye on her upset student. Both the coach and I knew who the child was and asked the teacher what had just occurred.

The teacher explained that after a small group of students made unkind remarks to this student, he stood up, went over to where they were seated, and was obviously going to punch one of them. The teacher turned around to see what was about to occur and yelled, "NO!" The student stopped, turned around, and walked out of the class.

The coach walked over to the student standing against the lockers and questioned him about what occurred in the classroom. As the coach asked questions and gave motivational statements, I watched the student's body language.

I tapped the coach's arm and said, "Coach, you can stop. He can't hear you."

The coach looked confused. I pulled him back and quietly stated, "He is emotionally unregulated. It's going to take him 30-40 minutes before he calms down and can have a rational conversation. Here, I will show you. Take a look at the student and his non-verbals."

With my back to the student and standing next to the coach, I told him to look at the following:

- Stiff body and posture
- Clenched fists
- Glossy eyes
- Heavy breathing
- Unresponsive to verbal cues

I asked, "So what does this behavior and nonverbal communication tell us?"

Coach looked at me and said, "He's here physically but not mentally."

"Exactly."

TENET 2: EXPLORE THE BREAKDOWN

Based on what we learned in Chapter 2, adverse childhood experiences (ACEs), trauma, and chronic stress have negative impacts on the body and the brain and can influence student learning and behavior. Functional Behavior Analysis (FBA) also gives us an established process to assess where behaviors may stem from as well. There is a lot to think about, and because we operate in a busy profession, we want to ensure you have a simplified approach to explore behavior solutions while considering the myriad underlying issues.

Administrators respond to a great deal of negative student behaviors. Educators we work with, are reporting that they are observing increased behavioral issues, especially among students who have a difficult time regulating their emotions and acting rationally under duress. Their teachers are struggling to meet student needs and manage a classroom under these circumstances.

As educators, we all learn the importance of Maslow's Hierarchy of Needs, but rarely do we discuss how to assist in our student's mental and emotional health using this framework. As the Ohio Department of Education states, the brain of a child who has been exposed to trauma at an early age develops quite differently and functions in "survival mode" at a higher percentage.[19] With this information, we can learn to meet their needs to intervene more effectively (see diagram below).

---

[19] https://education.ohio.gov/Topics/Student-Supports/School-Wellness/Trauma-Informed-Schools

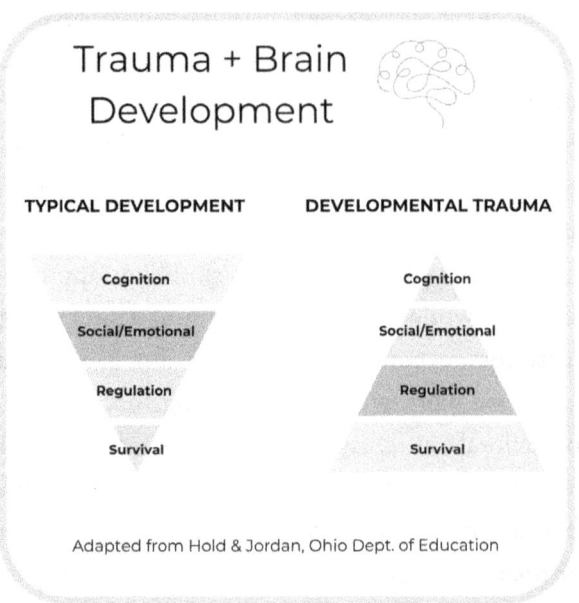

Adapted from Hold & Jordan, Ohio Dept. of Education

As described in Chapter 2, these students often go into "survival mode" where their prefrontal cortex—which is the area of the brain that creates logic and reason—goes "off-line"[20] and their limbic system—which is the lower functioning area of the brain—takes over. The brain is trained to survive dangerous situations and changes the function of the neurological system in times of hardship or stress. After repeated experiences of trauma and perpetual stress, the brain copes by operating at a primal level.

Examining Student Behavior

When dealing with high stress or adverse situations, all humans have three common responses that can occur: fight, flight, or freeze. Most of us know these by now, and the goal is to be astutely aware of the way

---

[20] This is language Dr. Daniel Siegel describes this process here https://drdansiegel.com/.

TENET 2: EXPLORE THE BREAKDOWN

our body and behavior subsequently respond. However, adults still feel overwhelmed when kids are disruptive and typically don't know what to do, so we resort to the same punitive measures we've always taken, or we do nothing at all. Both of these options typically worsen or prolong the situation.

In schools, where our kids spend much of their time and energy, we have students attending with various forms of unprocessed trauma and may even be experiencing adversity to varying degrees. With their underdeveloped brain and lack of life experience, they may go into a fear-based state quickly. With a shift into survival mode, the brain gets "emotionally hijacked" and those troublesome behaviors surface.

The language they're speaking to us is primal. Here are some examples of behaviors associated with each survival state that has an underlying:

Flight
- Skipping class
- Avoiding work or people
- Withdrawing from activities
- Fleeing the classroom
- Daydreaming
- Sleeping (or appearing to)
- Hiding under a desk
- Wandering around the halls
- Disengaging from the lesson

Fight
- Punching
- Arguing
- Acting silly
- Talking back
- Exhibiting defiance

- Posturing aggressively
- Using foul language
- Being hyperactive
- Screaming/yelling

Freeze
- Exhibiting numbness
- Refusing to answer
- Refusing to get needs met
- Giving a blank look
- Feeling unable to move
- Immobilizing

> *"...traumatic stress reactions are normal reactions to abnormal circumstances."* (SAMHSA, 2014)

When digging into the research, you may come across other less popularized trauma responses sometimes referred to as fawn, fright, faint, flag, flop. These may explain behaviors that leave us scratching our heads. Take the example of chronic absenteeism. This could be explained by a student feeling completely immobilized and struggling to get out of bed to attend school. It may be difficult to understand, and we may say to ourselves, "I would never let my kid do that," or "He's so spoiled!" However, adjusting our perspective will help us think something like this instead: "I wonder what happened to cause this?"

Shaming and punishing this behavior simply won't make it better, and, in fact, it could make matters worse. Rather than trying to serve our own needs to "get that kid to school" or "make that kid do their work," we can adopt a more productive mindset.

TENET 2: EXPLORE THE BREAKDOWN

Identifying the Manifestations of Trauma in Behavior

> One of our teachers was getting violently sick each day, and she asked for someone to cover her class with each episode. She was frustrated and felt extremely guilty asking other staff members to assist in her class. It seemed to occur after she ate meals throughout the day. This continued for several weeks until she went to the doctor for help.
>
> Every time she went to the doctor, they asked her to fill out several forms regarding physical history, allergies, and questions about what was occurring. It was quite an extensive and tedious process.
>
> When she was called back to see the doctor, the first step was to determine what was wrong based on her symptoms. The doctor would ask, "What hurts? When did the pain start? What occurred prior to you getting sick?" With each nurse, doctor, or specialist, she had to answer a vast number of questions about the symptoms and medical tests to determine the prognosis and a treatment plan.
>
> She lost a lot of weight and energy through the examination process and started to lose hope. After several weeks of many doctor visits and tests, they finally determined that her gallbladder needed to be removed. Within days of the diagnosis, she was in surgery and saw an immediate improvement as soon as the procedure was completed. Although the process took longer than expected, she was very happy with the result.

Similar to a doctor, we need to work together to decode a student's unusual or problematic behavior by looking at the "symptoms." Now, we're not asking you to be doctors or therapists, but we are asking you to shift from using unfair or snap judgments to being inquisitive.

Initial trauma responses can include "exhaustion, confusion, sadness, anxiety, agitation, numbness, dissociation, confusion, physical arousal, and blunted affect."[21] If a student witnesses a traumatic event like a car accident or domestic violence, for example, and then heads to school, imagine how these symptoms might show up in the hallway, classroom, or cafeteria.

Hyperarousal is another result of trauma that is the body's way of protecting itself from potential threats to come, which can last years after trauma occurs. If someone remains in this state, they might tense their muscles, experience sleep disruptions, or startle easily.[22] Think about how it must feel to be in this state and be scolded for having to "sit still!" "stop talking!" or "get working!" What about having to sit at an uncomfortable desk for most of the day or have little movement to allow the energy to release from your body and tension from your muscles? Our body (nervous system) is charged and may not be able to withstand this, so inevitably, there will be an eruption, somewhere at some point.

Misbehavior is a symptom of a deeper problem. It could be rooted in the student's negative experiences eliciting chronic stress or manifesting trauma. It is helpful to learn the history of the student, discover their "pain points," and document the incidents in which heightened emotions occur. Even with the guidance of the mental health team, we may never know what those underlying issues are, but we'll know they are there, contributing to disruption.

---

[21] Center for Substance Abuse Treatment (US). Trauma-Informed Care in Behavioral Health Services. Rockville (MD): Substance Abuse and Mental Health Services Administration (US); 2014. (Treatment Improvement Protocol (TIP) Series, No. 57.) Chapter 3, Understanding the Impact of Trauma. Available from: https://www.ncbi.nlm.nih.gov/books/NBK207191/

[22] Jovanovic et al. (2009); National Library of Medicine (2014)

TENET 2: EXPLORE THE BREAKDOWN

What we *can* do is:

- investigate
- lead with curiosity
- ask analytic questions

Documenting our observations and findings helps to identify patterns and make us valuable informants when we pass them on to mental health professionals for service. Educators may not be therapists but *are* essential members of the support team.

Additionally, when students exhibit strong emotions, which usually accompanies fractious behaviors, maintaining composure affords us the clarity to assess the issue holistically. In this state of mind, we have the capacity to ask:

- What happened?
- What are they trying to tell me?
- What do they need that they aren't getting?

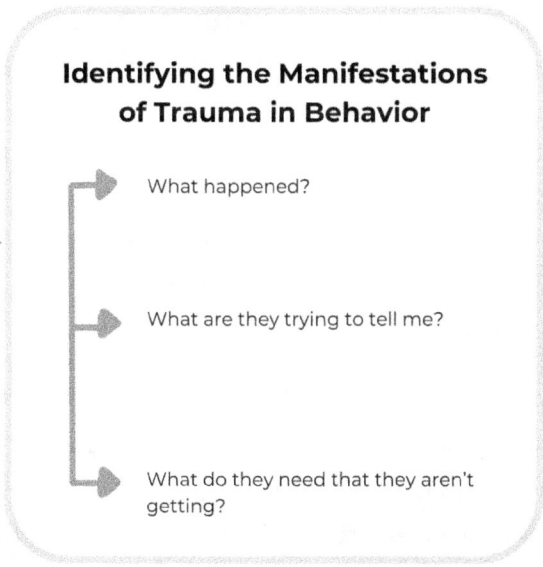

It's also constructive to learn their baseline and patterns of behavior. This happens when we have a connection to them, so calling on others for insight who have established relationships will save time and effort. We'll have a better understanding of "the big picture" and can better determine what is being communicated by the student. Once we know the message, we can respond by meeting their needs.

The following story is an example of this process.

> A middle school principal we worked with, Mr. Steinback, had a student, Emma, in his office frequently throughout the year for chronic misbehavior. Emma was always respectful and courteous to Mr. Steinback. With each interaction, he was confused and wondered why she was getting in trouble in her classes.
>
> Toward the end of the year, a teacher brought Emma to Mr. Steinback's office and explained that she refused to do any work.
>
> "Hey, what's going on?" Mr. Steinback asked with intrigue and concern.
>
> She looked down and said, "I'm just having a tough day."
>
> They didn't have a wonderful relationship, but Mr. Steinback felt like they had positive interactions throughout the school year, which may have resulted in a small amount of trust built. He decided he would ask more probing questions.
>
> "I'm confused. I don't know you well, but you seem to be a really nice person who has a ton of potential to be a successful adult. However, at school, you are sent to my office frequently for a variety of reasons. I just don't understand. Why is there such a drastic difference between the person who I speak with and the student in class?"
>
> She raised her head and said, "I just don't like school."
>
> Emma's nonverbals relaxed, and her responses became more engaged. Mr. Steinback continued to ask a variety of questions about her family dynamics, prior experiences in school, hobbies,

TENET 2: EXPLORE THE BREAKDOWN

future goals, and triggers to learn more about what was causing her anger. Based on her responses, he could tell there was a deeper issue going on in her life.

After about thirty minutes of conversation, Emma said, "I appreciate you talking with me today. Most principals just send me to ISS."

He smiled and replied, "Well, I am here to help you be the best version of yourself. Like I said before, I think you have the potential to do great things. You are going to have consequences for your behavior today, but we need to figure out what that is going to look like."

She looked down again and asked, "I've never told anyone this before, but can I share why I get so angry?"

"Of course," he responded–but, in hindsight, was not mentally prepared for Emma's response.

She began to cry and explained that several years prior, she was sexually assaulted by an extended family member who had recently moved back to the area. She was scared that it was going to occur again and didn't know what to do. It consumed her thoughts and distracted her from doing her work in class.

In shock, Mr. Steinback gently asked, "Who are the adults in this building you trust the most?"

She gave a counselor's and teacher's name, and just after that, the principal found coverage for both of them and called them into his office. After explaining the situation, they all worked together to determine a plan to keep Emma safe.

The rest of the day was devoted to finding the appropriate district resources for emotional support, communicating with all parties, getting law enforcement involved, and creating a wellness team to support this student on campus. This careful, intentional action may have just changed the trajectory of this student's life for the better.

This is a reminder that we don't always know what is occurring in the lives of our students. Many sit in our classrooms, cafeterias, and hallways ruminating about their horrific experiences and holding the emotional charge in their bodies. They move into their classes and are expected to concentrate on the lesson, explore new ideas, engage in social activities, and constantly be "on." That's tough for adults to do, so imagine the added strain for a child or adolescent with little to zero coping strategies.

They express their fears, anxiety, frustrations, anger, and other difficult emotions behaviorally–typically with reactivity. They aren't thinking, "I'm nervous about going home today to my alcoholic father, so I'm going to stare off into space and think of a plan to deal with it while Mrs. Smith is delivering her lesson." The more typical scenario has Mrs. Smith noticing the student avoiding her instruction to "get to work" and calls the student out. The student, feeling already charged and overwhelmed with stress hormones, gets shaken into reality, says something with an "off" tone (that the teacher doesn't like) and gets further reprimanded.

As teachers, counselors, social workers, school-based therapists, and administrators, we all have extremely busy schedules. However, it is crucial to take the time to get to know our students on a deeper level and to learn about them beyond the academic scope so we can give them some space and grace when we notice a shift in their baseline behavior. We'll respond like Mr. Steinback did and perhaps avoid the office referral altogether.

Looking back, it could have been a terrible situation if Mr. Steinback had just sent Emma to ISS without digging deeper and building a trusting relationship with the student. He may have been one more adult who let her down which could have made her spiral into hopelessness. This is a dark path to follow which can lead to more severe issues such as depression and suicidality. As educators, we must make time to:

TENET 2: EXPLORE THE BREAKDOWN

1. ask pivotal questions
2. assess responses
3. determine unmet needs

These simple, yet important, action steps will give us something tangible to do to support the student's needs. We don't have to be therapists to do this. We just have to remember to use this tool and have compassion while doing so.

Recognizing Behavioral Signs and Symptoms of Trauma in Students

If you have ever worked in a school, you probably have seen fight, flight, or freeze behaviors exhibited in various forms. The toughest and most frustrating part of classroom management is feeling like we've lost control or not knowing what to do. It might also be challenging to determine the root of a student's poor behavior—like trying to put together a puzzle with a bunch of missing pieces.

THE LANGUAGE OF BEHAVIOR

Each student is unique in their diverse experiences, and each child is parented differently with myriad cultural influences that may be in conflict with ours. We can't assume that each child understands or knows how to interact appropriately with adults or authority, especially in a highly emotional state. Our tactics with student behavior must be differentiated, the same as we do with academics. If we view behavior as a form of communication instead of a personal quality or character flaw, the misbehavior has a purposeful function to determine the unmet need.

When investigating potential symptoms of trauma in students, it's essential to ask sensitive and thoughtful questions. Some key questions to consider regarding student behavior include:

- What are specific behaviors observed?
- What behavior changes are observed?
- When did these behaviors start?
- Have the behaviors become more frequent over time?
- Have the behaviors become more intense over time?
- Are there any significant events or changes in the student's life that coincide with the onset of these behaviors?
- How do these behaviors impact the student's classroom engagement?
- How do these behaviors impact the student's academic performance and relationship with teachers?
- How do these behaviors impact the student's peer relationships?
- How do these behaviors impact the student's overall well-being?
- Have there been any noticeable patterns or triggers associated with the behaviors?
- What coping strategies does the student employ when faced with challenging situations?
- What has worked in mitigating these behavior issues for this student in the past?

TENET 2: EXPLORE THE BREAKDOWN

- What risk factors does this student have?
- What protective factors does this student have?
- How does the student typically respond to support or interventions aimed at addressing these behaviors?
- Who is typically involved with this student's support and intervention?
- Are there any underlying factors, such as family dynamics, socioeconomic status, or cultural background, that may be contributing to this student's behavior?
- Have there been any previous experiences or traumas that could be influencing the student's current behavior?

It's essential to investigate with empathy, cultural sensitivity, and a commitment to creating a safe environment for all students. These questions can help administrators, teachers, mental health professionals, and support staff gain a deeper understanding of the underlying factors contributing to student behavior and tailor interventions and support accordingly. It's also a helpful tool to use while discussing prevention, intervention, and postvention strategies with parents and caregivers.

The Missing Puzzle Pieces

Let's play a quick game called "Guess that Word." Below is a series of four words with missing letters. You need to fill in the blanks to determine the correct word:

F_ _K
SH_T
_ELL
D_M_

Most people, when they see these four words, respond with either laughter or a gasp of shock. If, at first glance, the four words look inappropriate, you are not alone. However, the answers to the game are as follows:

FORK
SHOT
BELL
DIME

The "Guess that Word" game is a metaphor for what occurs on campuses every day. When we don't have all the information, it's easy to fill in the gaps with negative responses. It's human nature and happens every day in our lives as a way for our brain to protect ourselves from threats in our environment (commonly referred to as negativity bias or risk aversion bias). Our amygdala is over responsive, which may distract us from reality. For example, have you ever sent a text to someone and they didn't respond immediately? What are your thoughts after sixty minutes have passed with no response? What about after three hours?

"Oh, I guess I'm not important."
"Looks like I'm getting ghosted."

Now, I want you to think about the student who puts his head down as soon as they sit down at their desk, or the girl who won't stop talking throughout class, or the student who constantly asks to go anywhere in the school other than your class. What are our thoughts about them?

"They hate my class."
"Man, they are trying to make my life difficult."
"That kid is just a bad kid."

TENET 2: EXPLORE THE BREAKDOWN

These are not uncommon thoughts; however, we must be intentional about filling the missing pieces of the story with positive intent and empathy. When we find out why we didn't get a text response back from our friends or family, it is typically due to something that was much more urgent and required their time and attention elsewhere. Similar to the text message example, the student's action has a story and often it is due to something much deeper than their annoying, withdrawn, or loud behaviors.

Slow Build

Change takes time. Some people have an epiphany or traumatic event that convinces them to make an immediate behavioral change. An example of this is one who overdoses and chooses a path of sobriety by checking into rehab. Still, the change process is about altering habits and patterns we've grown accustomed to, which become reflexive practice. We get some kind of benefit from that go-to behavior, whether it's to mask emotional pain or feel a rush of sensation after feeling numb. That's why there is a long journey ahead for the person who checked themselves into rehab, even after deciding they want to live differently. They lose the payoff and have to find a better replacement.

In order for the new behavior to stick, it's best to take incremental steps. A common issue we see in schools is chronic absenteeism. In order to help a student process the underlying cause, therapeutic intervention is helpful along with a plan to implement a "baby steps" approach back to the classroom. Once that student progresses through each step (e.g., getting out of bed and dressed for school), encouragement is crucial. Celebrating small wins will eventually result in monumental outcomes, especially when family and school members fully engage in the process.

We're not saying change is easy. In fact, it's evident that it is not. A review of studies with neuroscience underpinnings and a focus on motivation, reward learning, executive function, and self-relevance demonstrated complex behavior change in two dimensions: the *will* (motivation) and the *way* (cognition).[23] Ultimately, it showed that achieving a new behavior involves the level of effort it takes to achieve change, our desire to change, and the skills and knowledge to do so.

A Team Effort

Everyone plays a role in student behavior intervention. For example:

> A *student* accepts that they need a change and enters a contract.
> A *therapist* can help the student process the event and emotions underlying the cause.
> A *caregiver* can transport their kid to appointments and relay information to others.
> A *counselor* can outline accommodations and work with teachers to implement them in the classroom.
> A *social worker* can advocate for the student and connect them to community resources.
> A *teacher* can employ the accommodations and break large projects into smaller steps.

Because we know change will take time, we approach it with compassion, understanding, and collaboration. We can serve students as an entire support team without the solution feeling too big for any one person. Remember, kids want to appear competent and want to *be* and *do* well. Sometimes they need additional support to get them there. If we simplify our thinking and avoid taking their behavior personally, we can respond to their needs with more intentionality to mitigate the issue more favorably.

---

[23] Berkman (2018). Read the full journal article here https://www.ncbi.nlm.nih.gov/pmc/articles/PMC5854216/

TENET 2: EXPLORE THE BREAKDOWN

When we seek understanding and decode the message underlying the behavior and lean on each other in collaboration, we can turn our focus to simply meeting a child's unmet need(s). Intentional and logical actions, emotional connection, and a team effort all contribute to a more desirable outcome.

Implementing Tenet #2

Jamie, a kindergarten student, refused to go to school after only a week of attending. Following conversation with his mother, the administrative team learned that Jamie had been excited about coming to school initially. He also behaved well at home and was consistently compliant with his parents' requests. It was clear that something had changed his mind.

Jamie's teacher reported that Jamie rolled around on the carpet while other students obediently sat in their designated space at circle time. Using a visual behavior chart, the teacher moved Jamie's green card to yellow, and finally to red after reminders to sit in the "criss cross applesauce" position. When that news was shared with Jamie's parents, they were noticeably beside themselves. Jamie had low muscle tone which made it difficult to sit in the cross gross position. This wasn't disclosed to his teacher, and without this pertinent information, his teacher assumed that Jamie was "being silly." Jamie felt humiliated when his yellow or red card stood out among all the other children's green cards. In anticipation of this occurring again and again, Jamie grew extremely anxious.

Uncovering deeper factors that contribute to misunderstood behaviors in students (like Jamie) takes an intentional multifaceted method. We need to consider their history and other pertinent factors such as family situation, peer influences, and negative experiences. Here are some strategies to uncover these factors and implement Tenet #2:

THE LANGUAGE OF BEHAVIOR

1. Use What You Already Know

   + **History:** What is this child's history that might help us take quick action? (e.g., they are diabetic and need insulin or they have ADHD and need movement).
   + **Past Success:** What has worked well for this child before (in this setting or other settings)?
   + **Strengths:** What strengths does this child have that we can utilize? Do they have soothing strategies that typically work well for them that they are willing to use? (e.g., box breathing, coloring)
   + **Empathetic Listening:** Listen to understand students' perspectives and experiences (Peck & Caswell, 2023). Encourage them to express themselves freely without fear of judgment. Listen attentively to verbal and nonverbal cues to gain deeper insights into their emotions and motivations.
   + **Trauma and ACEs:** Remind yourself that their behavior comes from a physiological response that manifests in the brain. This will help you remain calm and compassionate while pursuing an intentional response.
   + **Developmental Capacity:** We know that children lack skills and life experience. Remember to meet them where they are in their growth and learning stage, and accept that they are lacking the skills and knowledge to comply at an adult level.

2. Conduct a Brief Inquiry

   + **Observation:** Pay close attention to non-verbal cues, behaviors, and interactions in different contexts, such as the classroom, playground, and social settings. Observe patterns, changes of behavior, and triggers that may communicate a hidden need or resource.

TENET 2: EXPLORE THE BREAKDOWN

- **Rapid Research**: Use this framework. There might be a simple solution to meet this child's need to resolve the issue quickly. This may also prevent escalation and bypass a more onerous intervention (see the "Rapid Research: Decoding Behavior" graphic above).

3. Dig Deeper

- **Gather Important Information**: Look at records, surveys, assessments, and any other pertinent documents that might help to make sense of the underlying problem.
- **Utilize Multiple Sources**: Speak with the student, parents/guardians, caregivers, coaches, and other school staff members. They may provide valuable insights into students' home life, personal challenges, and past experiences that influence their challenging behavior.

Take Action

Assess the process of how you currently work through student behavior and ask the following questions:

- What steps are involved in decoding student behavior incidents?
- Is your staff trained to determine flight, flight, and freeze behaviors?
- Are there clear protocols or procedures in place for handling various types of student behavior and emotional regulation?
- Is there collaboration among teachers, counselors, social workers, and other support staff?
- Do educators have the opportunity to build rapport and trust with students during the behavior resolution process?

- Is there adequate time built into the process to address underlying issues and build a relationship with the student?
- How are parents or guardians involved in the process, if at all?
- Is there a system in place for monitoring and tracking changes in student behavior, past incidents and affective resolutions?
- Are there opportunities for reflection and improvement in the behavior resolution process?

Once these questions are answered, your team can determine what areas need to improve regarding student behavior response protocols, additional professional development, and resources provided to assist students who have experienced trauma, chronic stress, or extreme adverse situations.

CHAPTER 4

Tenet 3: Respond Intentionally

"It's not about managing your emotions, it is about managing your reaction to your emotions."

–Yung Pueblo

It was February, the month with one of the highest number of discipline infractions and referrals, and we had student after student sent to In-School Suspension (ISS). Our room wasn't large enough to hold the expanding number of students, and the ISS clerk was extremely overwhelmed. Teachers reported feeling frustrated that ISS wasn't helping to alter student behavior or getting them to be more successful academically like they'd hoped.

If you're a school leader, have you ever experienced a situation in which staff members were upset by how you handled discipline issues? Maybe you are a teacher who disagreed with an administrator and questioned their approach. Think about that sinking feeling you might have after reviewing the monthly discipline data sheet littered with student infractions or witnessing an ineffective behavior management tool which actually escalates behavior. As you read this chapter, we want to provide you with a plan for establishing a different system in your school or classroom. It is designed to help students:

- regulate their emotions.
- reflect on their choices.
- learn desired behavior.

Below, we'll introduce transformative exercises that can be used to shift perception about student behavior. Based on the ineffective use of ISS, OSS, and repeated discipline practices, it is evident that sometimes our current approach isn't achieving the outcomes we desire. Instead of rectifying student behavior, existing systems may exacerbate the very issues they were trying to address. As an administrator, Joshua remembers a time when his campus leaders hadn't yet been effective with behavior management and desperately needed a shift in perspective. There was a precise moment in which he realized that they needed to respond more intentionally:

> Joshua was in the early years of leadership. His administrative team commissioned a local regional team to implement a campus-wide Positive Behavioral Interventions and Supports (PBIS) system. On the first day of training, their professional development (PD) team facilitated a whole staff training onsite and brought the admin team into their cafetorium. It had four large sections that inclined to different levels, and all members of the team stood at the top level.
>
> The regional leader provided directions to staff: "If you never went to the principal's office as a student in your educational K-12 experience, please go to the lowest level."
>
> About 97% of the staff moved to the lowest level.

TENET 3: RESPOND INTENTIONALLY

> He continued, "If you went to the principal's office once, please move to the next level."
>
> Around 1% of the staff went and stood at the next level.
>
> "If you went to the principal's office twice in your educational career, please move to the third level."
>
> 1% of staff moved to stand on that level.
>
> "If you went to the principal's office three or more times in your educational career, please stay at the top level."
>
> The remaining 1% of staff continued standing on the top level as the rest of the 99% looked up at them.
>
> It was glaringly obvious that the vast majority of staff had never gotten caught cheating, physically fought in the hallway, skipped school, or got in trouble for a variety of other serious infractions. It was clear that the teachers' own school experiences as children were positive and successful. They thrived academically and successfully navigated their educational journeys. Now as adults, they longed to work in the system that they enjoyed so much as students. However, after reflecting on this activity, teachers realized they struggle to connect with students who want nothing to do with school because the teachers didn't have any issues themselves as students and lacked that critical perspective.

Addressing Core Needs

The need to change the way student discipline issues were resolved became apparent. Josh didn't have all the answers as the building leader, and he knew it. Several staff members continued to share their concerns about student behavior and wanted harsher punishments (including corporal punishment), expulsion, and extended isolation. It was evident that a "top-down initiative" would fail because many teachers were not in the mindset to adopt new practices. After speaking to several staff members about the current campus climate and increased behaviors, we decided to form a group to explore a new approach. We invited seven people, including teachers, counselors, administrators, and others who held various leadership roles. The purpose was to learn and try new strategies. We decided to call the group *The Relationship Action Team*, which eventually, and unfortunately, was nicknamed the *R.A.T.s Group*.

The Relationship Action Team

This group of like-minded educators was invited to join because each participant saw there was a campus-wide need for change, and they each were open to exploring different, unorthodox practices. The R.A.T.s group met every two or three weeks to explore and learn about new classroom tactics, behavior management strategies, and communication tips. During our first meeting, we created three core norms for the group that would guide us to grow from the seven founding participants to almost half our staff by the end of the school year.

One thing we know for sure is that the education system is changing, and teachers are really struggling with student behaviors. They are trying their best but wish they had more practical tools to work with. Here are anonymous social media posts we keep seeing with only slightly different wording:

"I don't think I can do another nine years [of teaching]!!! I don't think I can do this year yet alone another nine! This is not what I signed up for twenty-one years ago. I worry about the difference I truly make on a daily basis."

"Debating on leaving teaching after this school year…if I even have it in me to finish the year. Every year the students get more and more out of control. I feel like I'm running a daycare."

TENET 3: RESPOND INTENTIONALLY

Having a team to continually research new ways of approaching the challenging issue of managing student behavior is crucial to adapting to changing needs and circumstances. Teachers are trying! They're disheartened and overwhelmed so we need to have a dedicated group to continually support them that will subsequently benefit kids. Let's start with some parameters. As a grassroots movement, the R.A.T.s group created group norms. They are:

1. *Be open-minded.*
   We all bring our own past experiences, biases, and beliefs to the table. For this team to be successful, we need to check all those potential distractions at the door and be receptive to information and strategies shared within the group.

2. *Attempt new strategies in your classroom and school with vulnerability.*
   It's one thing to review new research, philosophies, and evidence-based practices (EBP), but it's another to implement them successfully in an educational setting. Most of the R.A.T.s participants were fearful of trying something new because they didn't want to fail, lose control of the group, or appear weak in front of their students. It was imperative to make an attempt, though, and if they were successful, they could adopt the new strategy in their classroom practice immediately. If they were unsuccessful, then it was clear it wasn't a fit for the teacher or our campus.

3. *When something works, share it with a colleague and invite them to be in the R.A.T.s group.*
   Too often, teachers perform marvelous and effective tactics every day, and no one ever knows about them. Breaking down the "teacher silos" on campus and increasing communication among staff is paramount to growth and success.

Action-based steps established by the R.A.T.s team include:

1. Communicate all the strategies that work well.
2. Detail specific results the strategies produced.
3. Invite colleagues to a future meeting to learn more.

Action-Based Steps to Relationship Action Team

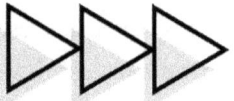

- Communicate all the strategies that work well.
- Detail specific results the strategies produced.
- Invite colleagues to a future meeting to learn more.

The last core norm was imperative to the success and growth of this group because it allowed neighboring teachers to engage in conversations about practical and successful behavior strategies, while providing an opportunity for them to learn more in a safe space with their peers in the R.A.T.s group. With teachers feeling empowered to try new strategies, determining what works for their students, and having evidence of effective practices, teachers were excited to share their successes and invite others to participate in the group. The enthusiasm and excitement was infectious, and the group attendance grew quickly.

TENET 3: RESPOND INTENTIONALLY

The First Strategies Implemented

During a R.A.T.s session, a counselor shared this story and expressed her frustrations about the way students were handled:

The counselor, Mrs. Hendricks, was walking down the 8th grade hall and saw a student and a teacher agitated with each other. When Mrs. Hendricks asked if she could step in, the teacher explained the series of events and how the student struggled to get his work done all throughout the morning.

The student yelled, "Forget this!" and hurried down the hall away from them.

Mrs. Hendricks called out to the student, "Hey, hold up!" and followed them down the hallway.

The student went straight to the counselor's office and flopped down in a chair. He put his face in his hands and began to sob. Mrs. Hendricks provided space for the student to cry and express his frustration. As soon as he gained composure, she encouraged him to take his time pulling himself together, do some breathing exercises, and head back to class when ready. Now, in a more stabilized emotional state, the student was able to tell Mrs. Hendricks about the chaotic events that occurred the night before, which included the police being called to his house.

Due to the evening events, he didn't get much sleep and was emotionally spent. As soon as he got off the bus at the start of the school day, the student didn't want to talk with anyone, learn, or be there at all. He pulled his hood up, made it to first period, and immediately put his head down on his desk.

The teacher felt heartbroken when Mrs. Hendricks provided an update. "I wish I would have known. I wouldn't have pushed him so hard to work this morning."

The counselor shared with the group, "We must understand that for many of our students, learning is not their first priority. Surviving is the most important thing."

After hearing this story, the first area of interest for the group was behavior *prevention*, starting with building healthy relationships. Next was to learn how to de-escalate situations and then to help students meet their basic needs. The focus question was:

How can we maintain self-control in order to be proactive with students?

The initial strategies implemented are discussed below, which became staples on campus for years:

1. **Greeting Students at the Door**

One of the first tactics was something familiar to many in the group. The strategy was to stand at the door and greet every child as they entered the classroom. As the Journal of Applied Behavior Analysis[24] states, greeting students at the door of the classroom, using their name, making eye contact, and offering a nonverbal greeting increases academic engagement by 20 percent and decreases disruptive classroom behavior by 9 percent. This strategy was occurring in various classrooms but not with consistency and intentionality. After reviewing the research, the R.A.T.s group vowed to make this a daily practice at their classroom door. The teachers who executed this in their daily practice reported that they saw immediate results:

- Healthy relationship created and/or maintained.
- Less interruptions and redirections during the lesson.
- Increase in attentive behavior and positive interactions.

---

[24] Allday, R. A., & Pakurar, K. (2007) More information can be found here: https://www.ncbi.nlm.nih.gov/pmc/articles/PMC1885415/

TENET 3: RESPOND INTENTIONALLY

Talk about an improved classroom culture! Students were craving human connection. Having their teacher present at the door, greeting them with a smile and using their name, helped build a positive relationship with their students and increased overall engagement.

2. Daily Check-Ins

Many of our students come to school each day with complex problems, chronic stress, and unhealed trauma. As educators, we need to find out how students are feeling and coping prior to delivering any kind of lesson, and we need to do so in a non-threatening way.

The R.A.T.s group discovered a strategy called a Daily Check-In from *The Restorative Practices Handbook for Teachers, Disciplinarians, and Administrators* authored by Bob Costello.[25] This strategy is a way for students to communicate what is going on in their lives, how they are feeling, and share if they need any additional resources. For example, when a student puts their head down on their desk, a teacher may be inclined to say, "Emma, put your head up and get to work." But what if we discovered that Emma didn't get any sleep the night before because the police were called to her home at 2:00 a.m. for a domestic disturbance between her mom and dad? Would we change the way we interacted and communicated with this student then?

The way many R.A.T.s teachers implemented the Daily Check-Ins was through a discreet electronic form to provide students a way to communicate how they were feeling through a number system (1-10) or color system. In addition, it allowed students to share what they needed to be successful. If they were hungry or wanted to speak to a counselor because they were having self-harming thoughts, for example, they had a way to communicate their needs to a trusted adult.

---

[25] Costello, B. (2009). *The restorative practices handbook: For teachers, disciplinarians, and administrators.* International Institute for Restorative Practices.

This strategy allows teachers to gain a deeper understanding of what is happening in the lives of students and address the deep-rooted problems impeding their learning. We didn't ask teachers to be therapists or social workers; rather, we had a team process that connected them to resources and support.

Establishing consistent time to build trusting relationships with students is crucial for gaining insight into their thoughts, feelings, and experiences. When students feel safe, comfortable, and supported, they are more likely to open up about their current challenges, emotions, and behaviors. Use these check-in opportunities to build rapport, address concerns, and offer guidance and support.

3. Treatment Agreements

The treatment agreement[26] is a collaborative activity with the class (or with a select group of students) to create shared expectations between all parties:

- student to student
- teacher to student
- student to teacher

The agreements are created to provide students an opportunity to have input and ownership in behavioral expectations. The relationship agreement is a working document, which has the opportunity to be changed and modified throughout the year. Teachers placed posters on the wall or laminated agreement sheets on student desks as daily reminders for both students and the teacher. Many days, students would respectfully police themselves by pointing out that another student's behavior or interaction wasn't meeting the relationship agreement.

---

[26] Borrowed from the National Educators for Restorative Practices (https://stephen-murray-nedrp.squarespace.com/cttreatmentagreement)

TENET 3: RESPOND INTENTIONALLY

STAFF TREATMENT AGREEMENT

These agreements can be adapted in any kind of relationship (e.g., parent to child, coach to player, supervisor to employee) so get creative with this strategy.

4. Affective Statements

In many of our walkthroughs, we heard teachers use common (and sometimes harsh) statements like, "Sit down, and be quiet!" "Stop teasing her!" or "What's your problem?" It's important for students to understand that language and actions affect our emotions and model how we identify and communicate how we feel. Affective statements are an alternative to these typical responses to behavior and can be expressed positively or negatively.

THE LANGUAGE OF BEHAVIOR

For *undesirable behavior* we want to stop:

- Include a feeling we get while witnessing the behavior.
- State the undesirable behavior we'd like them to stop.

EXAMPLE:

Instead of saying, "Stop teasing her," say, "I feel sad when I hear you tease Sarah like that."

Tone is important. We can be firm and kind at the same time. For younger kids, sometimes more animation or expression makes a stronger impact. We like to extend this using "I need" to foster empathy and model advocacy:

"I need you to keep unkind thoughts to yourself."

We can also encourage the student being targeted to ask for what they need, which we'll demonstrate in the example below.

For *positive behavior* we want to reinforce:

- Include a feeling we get while witnessing the behavior.
- State the desirable behavior we'd like them to keep doing.
- Tell them the benefit of that behavior.

EXAMPLE:

Let's say you see Isaiah run into another student, Ariel, in the hallway, sending her books scattering onto the floor. You then see Isaiah put his hand gently on Ariel's shoulder, mouth the words, "I'm so sorry, are you OK?" Isaiah then bends down and picks up all of Ariel's fallen books, handing them to her one-by-one.

You walk up to Isaiah and Ariel and say, "I am happy that you took the time to ask Ariel if she was OK after bumping into her. It shows you are concerned that you may have hurt her and care enough to make her feel better by picking up her books. Well done!"

We like to extend this with an "I need" statement.

Now let's say Isaiah bumped into Ariel and said he was sorry, then continued on down the hallway. You might say, "Hey Isaiah. I am happy you said you're sorry to Ariel. It shows you are concerned that you may have hurt her." Then you turn to Ariel and ask, "Is there anything you need from Isaiah?"

"Yes!" says Ariel. "I need him to pick up my books!"

You say, "Kindly tell that to Isaiah, Ariel."

"I need you to pick up my books please, Isaiah," Ariel says.

Here, we're building empathy and encouraging self-advocacy.

Be sure to adapt developmentally-appropriate wording, and be clear and concise when guiding behavior.

5. Investment Conferences

Sometimes we have a tough time making connections with certain students who seem disconnected to the classroom. It may be because we don't have similar interests, the communication is awkward, or the student is distant or disengaged. To create a healthy relationship with the student, we implemented the "Investment Conference," an intentional time designated to learn more about specific students.

Time Frame
Two minutes every day (per student) for two weeks.

Fitting It In
Schedule independent work time into each lesson over the two-week period.

2 minutes x # of students = independent work time

Not enough time? Reduce it to ninety seconds per student. The key is to be consistent and predictable so set a timer. Also, be fair with your time per student. Avoid spending five minutes with a student and one minute with another. It will scream favoritism, creating distrust. That negates everything.

Format

Informal, nothing fancy. Just a quick meet up at the teacher desk.

1. Ask: *How are you feeling?*
2. Ask three low level, get-to-know-you questions.
3. Ask: How are you feeling *now?*

Getting them to name their feelings helps them make sense of their emotions and normalizes the act of stating how they feel. This supports growth and development. It also strengthens connection and improves rapport, *as long as we're not judging or invalidating* their feelings. For example, if they say, "I'm frustrated," don't say, "You shouldn't feel that way." Instead, simply nod to communicate that you acknowledge their answer and have a safe space for them to openly share. Remember, this is a quick conference so there's no discussion around the feeling; we're simply giving them a chance to say it out loud.

EXAMPLE QUESTIONS:

1. What do you like to do for fun?
2. What's your favorite food? Drink?
3. What is something you're good at?
4. What is your favorite color?
5. What show are you into right now?

For older kids, or to make it more interesting, you could ask:

1. If you could have one meal for lunch every day, what would it be?

TENET 3: RESPOND INTENTIONALLY

2. If you were given a million dollars, how would you spend it?
3. Who would be the first person you'd tell a secret to?
4. Which celebrity do you wish you could meet?
5. If you could start a business, what product or service would you sell?

Norms

- Get down at the student's level.
- Set a timer and keep the same time for each student, every time.
- Allow answers to be optional. Encourage students to say what's "top of mind" if they're stuck, but they can also say, "Pass."
- Be consistent by starting and ending the same way.
- Be fair and spend the same amount of time with each student.

For example, always start with, "How are you feeling?" and end with, "How are you feeling *now*?"

This strategy is intended to show the student we care about them, want to *invest* in connecting with them, and are willing to build a more personalized relationship.

De-Escalation in Communication

As we all know, students are going to make mistakes and misbehave. When this occurs, how are we going to communicate to the students during a potentially chaotic time? Is our communication going to de-escalate the situation or escalate the student's emotions, expression, and behavior?

It's easy to assume that each child possesses emotional regulation skills but, unfortunately, many children have been exposed to, or are living through, horrific situations and have never been taught how to deal with their emotions. They haven't yet mastered the ability to self-regulate when their amygdala goes on high alert. Their nervous system reacts and their instinct to survive, take refuge, gain power, or just seek comfort takes over all rational thought.

When interacting with students we don't know or haven't established relationships with yet, use the following techniques to assist in student management to develop a trusting and positive relationship:

Low Tone and Volume The tone and volume of our voice can drastically influence the dynamics of an interaction. Raising our voice (volume) may gain the attention of a child in a stable environment with a healthy, typical functioning brain, but with a child experiencing developmental trauma, raising your voice may be a sign of danger and could trigger a trauma response (as outlined in Chapter 2).

Our tone communicates our mood and state of being. If it frequently shifts, it may create a sense of chaos or instability which can also incite a trauma response. We want a consistently mild tone and volume so kids feel secure with us.

In all interactions, utilize a low and controlled tone of voice to provide a calm response to student behavior. The goal should always be to deescalate the situation and create a stable environment instead of unleashing our own emotions, which may include anger and frustration.

Space and Proximity It is natural to attempt to correct a student's behavior by using close proximity. Some of us believe that showing dominance by leaning forward, for example, asserts our authority. We might want to communicate, "don't mess with me," but if we're on the receiving end of that, it only makes us more defensive. We won't produce the results we want this way. Kids, especially those who come from unstable environments and have trauma, may express "big" emotions reactively when challenged.

When communicating with a student who has experienced trauma, it is important to make sure we don't get too close or move too quickly toward or around them. We need to be mindful of our non-verbals and our spatial awareness to disarm fear. Getting too close to a student in a fight or flight situation will only increase the survival response.

TENET 3: RESPOND INTENTIONALLY

In addition to proximity of space, we need to be mindful of proximity of height. Instead of hovering over a student during an interaction, which may scare or intimidate the child, try to get down to the same level as the student. Bending down, taking a seat, or keeling removes that fear and allows a child to feel empowered.

It's important to mention that we're not "tiptoeing" around our students or letting them "run the show." Rather, we're intentionally creating a secure environment so we can keep them, others, and ourselves safe. We're using our knowledge and understanding of the physiology connected to trauma and our stress response so we can disarm their inner alarm system. That way, we can respond efficiently to meet their needs while considering the safety needs of everyone involved.

Avoiding Power Struggles

Students who have experienced trauma may also have redefined perceptions of safety, danger cues, and trust, which will lead to seeking control of other situations (see below). It is critical to understand that the child is trying to protect themselves as they get bigger and louder, and their behavior is a direct reflection of this insecurity or outright fear.

It's not comfortable to witness this, though, and it can catch us off guard. Reacting, instead of intentionally responding, to students who are deregulating doesn't typically produce results we want, though when we're busy and aren't sure what to do, we engage and unwittingly contribute to the conflict.

Oftentimes, as we are in a hurry or are pulled in many directions, we fall into the trap of thinking "I am the adult," or "They just need to do what I tell them," and we react by attempting to assert our authority. We're disappointed when they aren't compliant and end up feeling powerless or intimidated ourselves. Then we go into fight or flight mode. Now we're in a battle of wills, and that simply isn't effective. Even worse, we may ruin relationships or tarnish our reputation, and both may be difficult to repair.

Instead of pursuing power with big motions, a loud boisterous voice, and a scoured face, it's best to acknowledge the behavior as a request to response mindfully by:

1. Identifying the unmet need.
2. Validating the child's experience and feelings.
3. Giving them clear expectations.
4. Using respectful communication.
5. Remaining consistent and predictable.
6. Helping them get what they need.

It can be simple. Sometimes, though, our ego gets in the way, or we are the ones who feel threatened. When we address our own insecurities and function as healthy, thriving individuals, we are more clear-headed, and remaining calm is entirely possible. This is great news because it means we actually do have immense power. We just need to use it responsibly and with a clear intention.

Historically, schools operated on a punitive level for student behavior, which ignored finding a solution for students' mental health and often caused further trauma. Thankfully, many schools are now finding ways to incorporate restorative practices and social/emotional learning in classrooms. It is imperative we continue to focus on connecting and empowering our students by modeling, facilitating, and developing positive relationships. As educators, it is our responsibility to explore alternative strategies to break the cycle of trauma instead of relying on traditional approaches. Students won't be able to grow academically or realize their full potential until they consistently feel safe, respected and loved.

Use Resets Conflict doesn't always have to *feel* big and *get* big. If we catch someone in the midst of misbehavior or in the beginning stages,

TENET 3: RESPOND INTENTIONALLY

we can try to resolve it quickly with two reset techniques: Rapid Resets and the Reset Button.

Rapid Resets Using Rapid Resets (Peck & Cameron, 2023) intentionally shifts the energy, focus, and mood of an individual or a whole group. They are strategies to distract the amygdala and take only seconds to work.

EXAMPLE

When we notice signs that someone is "offline"[27] and misbehavior may occur, we playfully respond with the Finger-Thumb Switch that distracts the amygdala, gets people laughing, and brings people back to baseline. This helps to bring their brain back "online" so they can access the thinking and reasoning part of their brain.

How to do the Finger-Thumb Switch[28]:

> Put your left thumb up (like you're giving a "thumbs up"). Stick out your right pointer finger towards your left thumb. In a simultaneous motion, quickly switch to opposite positions—stick out your left finger at your right thumb. This will take practice, but eventually, you'll train your brain to do it in a swift, seamless motion. This is great to do before starting a task where you need to be laser focused like learning a complex topic, taking a test, playing a game.

The Reset Button Ms. Brousseu, a school counselor, talks with Leah, a nine-year-old who was sent to the office after snapping at the teacher when told to start a lesson. She claims she didn't hear the instructions and appears irritated and lethargic. Ms. Brousseu knows Leah well and remembers that she sometimes misses breakfast when left on her own

---

[27] Dr. Daniel Siegel demonstrates his idea of "Flipping Your Lid".
[28] Improving School Mental Health: The Thriving School Community Solution. (Peck, & Cameron, 2023, pg. 79)

before school because her mother works the night shift. Ms. Brousseu gives Leah some fruit, milk, and a granola bar and notices a boost in her mood several minutes later. "I'm sorry, Ms. Brousseu, I'm not sure why I did that," she says. "It's, OK, Leah. Set your reset button, and let's head back to class." Leah giggles as she pushes the imaginary button on top of her head.

Envision a button on top of our head that can be pressed to give us a redo or a reset. This indicates that it's time to move on and start anew after an incident. It shows forgiveness has taken place and helps kids realize that they have a chance of trying something more effective next time.

Foundations of Behavior Change

It is important to conclude Tenet 3 by reiterating the need to focus on positive recognition of behavior. Teaching new behavior, and providing alternate, replacement behaviors is foundational to improving student outcomes.[29] To keep the process simple, remember to be specific with behavior expectations you want to see, and use clear, straightforward language. It's OK to ignore some of the behaviors you don't want to give attention to, and many consequences of behavior will come naturally. These can be explored with students as a means to intentionally guide them through reflection and growth. Implementing consequences can be beneficial in order to hold students accountable for their actions, too, which can be impactful—especially when you have established trust and rapport. When considering the overall success of the student, the real goal is to make every effort to maintain a connection with them. That's when the magic happens.

---

[29] Dr. Jon Lee, personal communication, January 9, 2025.

TENET 3: RESPOND INTENTIONALLY

Take Action

As a school leader, "responding intentionally" does not mean you need to take on the responsibility to create a Relationship Action Team, a discipline committee, or restorative task force of any kind. However, we would advise you to look at your classroom, your grade level, or your campus to identify the following question: What are you, as the educator, able to control to remain proactive with your student's behavior? Once this question is answered, explore the strategies below to synthesize what you just read in this chapter:

- Determine what can be implemented immediately to understand what is occurring in the lives of your students
- Use R.A.T.s team core principles
- Be open-minded
- Attempt new strategies
- When something works, share it
- Greet students at the door
- Conduct daily check-ins
- Use Treatment Agreements
- Use affirmative language
- Engage regularly in investment conferences
- Consider your tone, volume and space to de-escalate and avoid power struggles
- Use resets to start fresh and move on

Ultimately, we want to create positive relationships and provide the appropriate resources needed for kids to be successful. As Joshua always states in his keynotes, "To get knowledge to the brain, you have to go through the heart."

Our students need to understand that as a teacher, counselor, social worker, or administrator, you care about them and their personal wellbeing. They are not just a test score, attendance rate, or GPA. The educational environment needs to show students that they are unique and wonderful individuals, who are a valuable piece to the community.

You'll definitely want to dive into the next chapter as we challenge traditional discipline methods across a spectrum of behaviors, and offer solutions that may help transform your entire school culture. Though we understand behaviors can be complex, oftentimes there are shifts we can all make that drive change.

PART II

The Road Ahead

CHAPTER 5

Transforming Discipline Practices

"It is powerful for our children to know that they are loved and adored even in the midst of their worst behaviors."

–Dr. Karyn Purvis

Now that we've learned the 3 Tenets and have a plan to reduce and respond to misbehavior, let's look at the bigger picture. In order for the 3 Tenets to have a profound impact, we need to foster a culture of support around them. In this chapter, we explore new ways to transform your current system. We'll start with a brief discussion of In School Suspension (ISS) and Out of School Suspension (OSS), traditional school discipline practices.

In-School Suspension

During our time in education, we've found many flaws in the In-School Suspension (ISS) model. A typical scenario goes like this:

THE LANGUAGE OF BEHAVIOR

- A student misbehaves.
- The teacher sends the student to the office.
- The student gets assigned to ISS by the administrator.

The student, likely angry, is removed from the classroom, serves their time in ISS, and then returns to class. However, their behavior doesn't magically improve. In fact, their hostility toward the teacher grows, and re-entry to the classroom just invites more animosity. The teacher remains frustrated because nothing was resolved, and the behaviors continue. The student becomes more upset because they feel misunderstood and unwanted. It's a constant cycle of negativity that gets exacerbated.

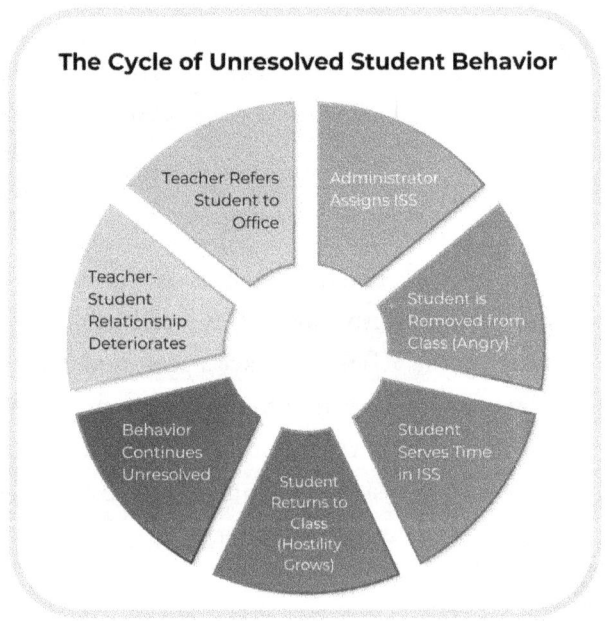

So who benefits from the ISS experience? Typically, no one. Here's why:

- Because of staff turnover or varied abilities for classroom management, there is inconsistency in the practices and procedures.
- Students enjoy the calm ISS workspace, feel less judged by the ISS teacher, and prefer this space to their classroom, so they'll act out to get back in there.
- Parents become upset about their kid being punished and missing so much instructional time.
- Teachers become upset because the student didn't complete the assigned work. This often creates more work, reteaching, and/or mental energy for them.
- The ISS room can be overcrowded which can cause more off task, negative behavior. This warrants additional consequences, and the cycle continues.
- After a student serves time in ISS, the behaviors continue when they go back to the same, unchanged environment.

An administrator we consulted in Arkansas experienced this frustration firsthand when a teacher approached her with clear disdain.

"ISS is a joke!" she lamented. "They don't do any work there. They just sleep or play games on their Chromebook. They should have to write one thousand sentences about what *not* to do and it should be a place they never want to be!"

This sentiment is shared by many overwhelmed educators who believe the punishment for misbehavior needs to be harsher. After listening to the teacher's complaint, the administrator explained the structure of ISS, gave a background of the student's circumstances, and asked the teacher, "Based on this new information, what do you think is the best alternative to our ISS system?"

The teacher was silent, visibly frustrated, and walked away without a solution. Later, the teacher explained they were frustrated because they wanted a quicker fix to the problem, which didn't add more time or energy to their already stressful responsibilities. They believed that ISS should be the solution and that harsher punishments should be placed on students by administration.

Educators tend to focus on their own situation and not systemic practices, which makes sense, but leaning heavily on administrators to fix student behavior issues isn't the answer. Together, we need to work to keep students in the classroom. The 3 Tenets will help with this, though remember, we're looking to strengthen the system around them for the best impact.

Keeping Students with the Content Expert

Frustrated and unsure of how to handle repeat offenders, teachers may send students to the office for minor infractions, such as disrespectful language or classroom distractions. Students can lose thousands of instructional minutes away from their content expert as a result, and when the punishment of ISS doesn't improve the student's behavior, more extreme measures, such as OSS or expulsion, may occur.

In the anecdote at the beginning of this book, Jacob was placed in ISS after a confrontation with Mr. Johnson. Maybe Jacob is a frequent ISS kid, with mounting behavior issues. Had he reacted more severely to Mr. Johnson, he may have received a harsher punishment such as an out of school suspension. Having him miss more class time may worsen his situation, and his grades may plummet. Researchers found in the past twenty-five years that out-of-school suspensions (OSS), exclusionary (ISS), and zero-tolerance discipline practices do not reduce or prevent misbehavior and actually correlates to lower academic achievement.[30] Let's take a look at the Out-of-School Suspension (OSS) approach, and then we'll offer alternative strategies.

Out-of-School Suspension

After examining research and reflecting on our own practices, it is evident that Out of School Suspension (OSS) is typically an ineffective tool for improving student performance. We continue to see a cycle of negative and repeated student behaviors, especially among students with complex trauma and high ACE scores, though there are certainly other contributing factors. OSS does not fix these underlying issues; rather, it creates more disconnection, animosity, and hostility for all parties involved. Balfanz and Boccanfuso (2007) found that students who are suspended and/or expelled from school were more likely to be held back a grade or drop out of school altogether.[31] Furthermore, the likelihood of being involved in the juvenile justice system increases dramatically. In fact, the single largest predictor of later arrest among adolescent females is having been suspended, expelled, or held back during their middle school years.[32]

Worse, vulnerable kids are put more at risk without proper guidance and protection as in the case of Kesha shared below:

---

[30] Hannigan, J. D., & Hannigan, J. E. (2022), p 6.
[31] Balfanz, R., & Boccanfuso, C. (2007)
[32] Wald, J., & Losen, D. (2003)

> Kesha, a 15-year-old female, lived with her mother who worked the night shift and was often too overwhelmed with her own mental health to parent her daughter. Kesha was suspended for vaping and sent home for several days. Without supervision, Kesha spent much of her time on her phone speaking with older men online, liking the attention. She sent topless pictures of herself to one particular man and hinted at a meet up, unsure if she had the nerve to actually follow through.
>
> Knowing Kesha was home alone, the man showed up at her door in broad daylight and assaulted her.

Unfortunately, kids like Kesha are left to navigate the world all on their own. Without supervision and reinforcement of their value and self-worth, teens like Kesha get cast aside and fall into dangerous situations, lacking guidance.

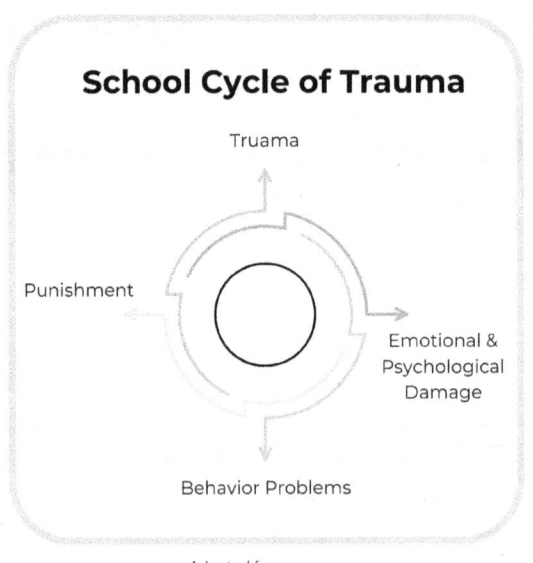

Adapted from source. [33]

---

[33] McInerney, M., & McKlindon, A. (2014)

Let's remove this high-risk component for a moment and review ISS and OSS in terms of learning outcomes.

One piece of evidence that stands out comes from John Hattie's ground-breaking influence ranking study where he developed a way of synthesizing various influences in different meta-analyses according to their effect size. In his ground-breaking study, he ranked 138 influences related to learning outcomes ranging from *very positive effects* to *very negative effects*.[34] Hattie found that the average effect size of all the interventions studied was 0.40. Therefore, he decided to judge the success of influences relative to this "hinge point" in order to find an answer to the question "What works best in education?" (see graphic below with the study's list of negative effects to learning).

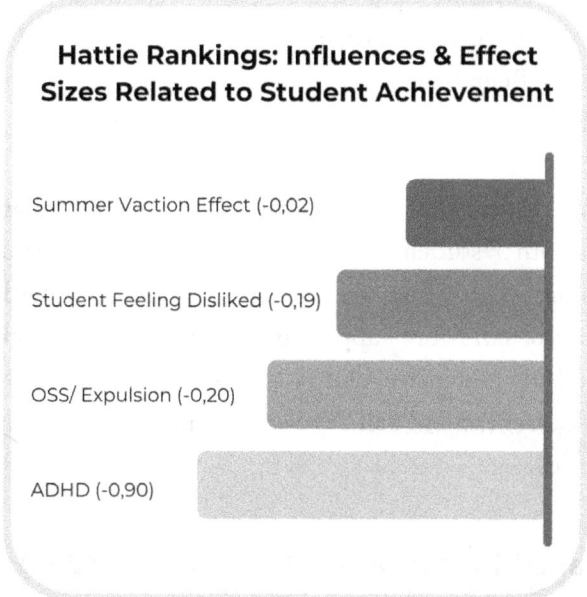

Source: https://visible-learning.org/hattie-ranking-influences-effect-sizes-learning-achievement/

---

[34] Hattie, John. "Hattie Ranking: Influences and Effect Sizes Related to Student Achievement." *Visible Learning*, https://visible-learning.org/hattie-ranking-influences-effect-sizes-learning-achievement/. Accessed 10 Oct. 2024.

Based on his research, Hattie determined that "suspension/expelling students," had one of the most negative effects on learning outcomes with a score of -0.20. Many of the negative influences on the graph above are outside the scope of control for the school. However, as we write this, suspensions and expulsions are common practice throughout the United States and viewed by many as an appropriate and productive form of punishment.[35]

Remember the R.A.T.s group introduced in Chapter 4? They collectively reviewed this research and posed the question, "Why are we doing the same thing over and over *if it doesn't work?*" Turning their attention to alternative ways to deal with student behavior issues, they found more effective solutions and leaned into providing more consequential outcomes and teaching to correct behavior. The transformation that occurred on their campus is what inspired us to share it with others. Below, we outline several models that we implemented successfully:

NOTE: We realize that some behaviors are aggressive and put the teacher and other students at risk; in such instances, we understand removal is necessary. There are deeper issues going on with the child that go unresolved. More support is warranted, such as school-based therapy or IOP (Intensive Outpatient Therapy) to help them build more self-awareness and self-regulation strategies particular to their circumstances.

Trust-Based Relational Intervention (TBRI)

Dr. Karyn Purvis, professor at Texas Christian University (TCU), teaches parents a variety of strategies through a program called

---

[35] Hannigan, Jessica Djabrayan, and John E. Hannigan. *Don't Suspend Me: An Alternative Discipline Toolkit.* 2nd ed., Corwin Publishing, 2022, p. 6.

TRANSFORMING DISCIPLINE PRACTICES

Trust-Based Relational Intervention (TBRI) that examines the "Time In" vs "Time Out" method.[36]

The "Time Out" discipline strategy was popularized in recent times and is used by many parents. The idea is to *remove* their child from an environment or situation after displaying poor behavior with the hope that the child will regulate their emotions, reflect on the situation, and change their behavior moving forward all on their own.

Purvis (2017) suggests that parents use a "Time In" approach to replace the traditional "Time Out" method which is more punitive. "Time In" is a similar strategy whereby the child still stops participating in the activity and is removed from the environment. However, the child remains with the adult so they can aid with regulation and avoid fracturing the relationship and evoking a power struggle which can escalate the behavior. Instead, the "Time In" strategy:

- allows the parent and the child to stay connected
- allows the adult to model regulation methods for the child
- seeks to understand the deeper problem
- creates space for the child to discuss ways their behavior affected those around them
- takes steps to resolve the issue.

By removing our kids away from our presence, we waste a valuable opportunity to proactively teach mercy, grace, and collaboration. When we are at our worst and feel like failures, we need someone to step in and say, "I love you. You're precious. Let's figure this problem out together."

As caregivers, we need to think about what the "Time Out" strategy communicates to our children and the subsequent long-term effects of sending our children away at a time they need our guidance the most.

---

[36] Purvis, K. and Cross, D. (2017). "Trust-Based Relational Intervention". Karen Purvis Institute of Child Development. https://texascasa.org/wp-content/uploads/2023/04/Instructor-Introduction-Overview.pdf

Discipline in the Classroom

How does this discipline strategy translate to the classroom? Well, the equivalent to a "Time Out" in schools is typically In-School Suspension (ISS). When a student exhibits poor behavior, we send them away and ask them to regulate themselves, on their own, and change their behavior moving forward–again, on their own. Are we hoping they'll be "fixed" from the ISS experience? Is the environment so rich and transformative that kids get the message and want to, and are capable, of immediate change? That's not typically the case, as we discussed earlier, though we're still seeing ISS used frequently as a way to address student misbehavior.

When a child makes a mistake at home, how long do we place the child in "Time Out"? Are they spending 4-8 hours in their room during this time? We hope not. Typically, the duration of time for a "Time Out" is much smaller, maybe 10-30 minutes, usually matching the child's age. However, in schools, we remove the students from the educational environment for up to eight hours, sometimes for multiple days. The "Time In" strategy can make a strong impact on student behavior prevention when used consistently.

The Push-In Model for Minor Infractions

This method incited radical change at the R.A.T.s group campus after learning about it from an administrator in St. Louis. Is it meant to:

- address small incidents that had little impact on others
- maintain a healthy, trusting relationship between the adult and student
- keep the student in the class to avoid missing instruction.

A Push-In method is used in schools already such as in co-teaching, differentiated instruction, ELL, and IEP services; however, the team was curious about how this would work in terms of behavior support.

They learned to use the Push-In method this way: when a student acts out, instead of sending a student to the office or to ISS, the teacher calls the office and requests a "Push-In." An administrator, counselor, coach, or social worker would then come to the class to take over for the teacher for a short period of time. This allows the teacher and the student to step outside the classroom or go for a walk to figure out the problem. During the Push-In, the teacher asks three important questions:

1. How are you feeling today?
2. What can I do to help you be successful in class today?
3. What are the expectations of the class and are you able to abide by them moving forward?

This tactic alleviated several stress points and was the main reason behind the decrease in ISS numbers and an increase in instructional time. Below are typical stress points and how this strategy alleviated them.

Push In Model
3 questions to ask

- How are you feeling today?
- What can I do to help you be successful in class today?
- What are the expectations of the class and are you able to abide by them moving forward?

Time A major complaint teachers report about student behavior is that they don't have time to address the issue during class. They have a whole group of students to manage and a lesson to deliver. The Push-In strategy allows other adults to "tag in," or rather "push in," and provides time for the teacher to focus their attention on one student. Though instruction is temporarily disrupted, only a few minutes are usually needed with the student 1:1 instead of having full blown chaos that disrupts the remainder of the entire class period. So in the grand scheme of it, little time is wasted and more meaningful time is spent understanding the issue often with resolve. It typically even prevents the behavior from occurring again.

Fractured Relationship When a student gets sent to ISS or the office, they frequently harbor feelings of animosity from being sent away. We hear students say things like, "My teacher hates me," or "They don't want me in their class." The misconception of ISS is that the behavior is wondrously going to resolve itself from the student's absence and the relationship between both parties will be intact. Clearly, this is not the case. Students and teachers come back together after ISS, still upset about the unresolved issue and previous conflict. They have hurt feelings, may be embarrassed, or have a guilty conscience without an outlet to express it. The Push-In model affords the space for students to express their thoughts and feelings. It also allows them to understand that it isn't about getting in trouble; it is about helping them work through a difficult time and finding an appropriate solution *together*.

Learning Loss When a student is sent to ISS or the office, they usually don't finish much of their work. This is always a pain point and area of concern for teachers. It adds more to their workload when they have to later "chase" the student for missed work or generate a packet for them to complete. Even if the student is given time to work on it, they may not have the skill set or academic knowledge to be successful on their own, which is why they needed the teacher in the first place. In a traditional model, the ISS supervisor will provide support to the student, but they aren't equipped to teach every subject. Keeping students in the classroom or only stepping out for a fraction of the time, solves this problem.

Guiding Change: Three Steps to Shape Behavior

When a student comes into an administrator's office after getting in trouble elsewhere, a variety of emotions rush over them: fear, anxiety, anger, nervousness, distrust. During these high emotions, they tend to shut down, lie, or deflect responsibility to other students.

We often ask, "*What* were you thinking?" or "*Why* would you do that?" Instead, we need to be more intentional and use this one-on-one time with them to gain a clear understanding of what occurred, allow a secure space for them to take responsibility for their actions, teach them the appropriate behavior for the future, and restore any harm that was caused.

We created the PRP Model so you have something simple to refer back to the next time a student shows up at your office for a behavior issue:

> **Provide** a safe space to debrief with the student so they can be more open to taking ownership of their actions.
> **Reflect** for growth by identifying the short- and long-term effects of their behavior.
> **Plan** to restore any harm to a relationship, property, situation, etc.

1. Provide a Secure Space

The minute a student walks into your office, they need to feel safe and welcomed. It helps when they don't feel boxed in and overstimulated too. Think of a spa or a therapist's office. What do you envision? You're likely imagining calming colors, soothing sounds, uplifting quotes, and an open space with simple decor. This design is purposeful.

Consider how your space feels to others. When a student does show up dysregulated, it is helpful to guide the student to a relaxed state using self-regulation strategies. Afterall, if a student's brain is in fight, flight, or freeze mode, it's pointless to have a conversation because they will be unable to engage effectively, and we want to avoid escalation. If we think back to the introduction and consider the opening scenario with Jacob, think about how he felt when his intentions were questioned by Mr. Johnson. He quickly went into "fight" mode, typical for a developing young adolescent who was not thinking rationally. Rather, his emotions took over, and he resorted to a defensive stance.

TRANSFORMING DISCIPLINE PRACTICES

This would have been a prime opportunity for Mr. Johnson to model and teach a self-regulation strategy. In doing so, Jacob could feel more at ease in Mr. Johnson's presence, rather than dysregulated. He'd have a chance to *practice* a self-regulation strategy so he could access the thinking part of his brain in order to provide a rational explanation. The outcome could have been much more fruitful for both Jacob and his teacher. Below are some **strategies** you can try with kids to help them (and you) get regulated:

- Do Rapid Resets[37]
- Soften the lighting
- Get fresh air
- Drink ice water
- Name their emotion(s)
- Play soft, relaxing music
- Take a walk outside
- Give them an ice pack
- Guide breathing exercises
- Play in a Zen sand garden
- Allow space for movement
- Put out fidgets and manipulatives
- Lead mindfulness activities
- Play a cartoon or funny video
- Model visualization
- Write in a journal
- Sit in a bean bag or bouncy chair
- Sit in silence
- Provide reading materials

Also important in this step is rapport-building. If we already have a trusting relationship with a student, this part is easy. When they know,

---

[37] Peck & Caswell (2021)

like, and trust us (a sales strategy in the business world), they are more willing to talk openly. If they aren't there yet, here are a few things we can do to establish rapport:

- Respect their space, leaving plenty of room between the two of you
- Check your posturing. Avoid hovering, and don't use an authoritarian stance
- Lower your tone and rate of speech
- Listen with a genuine intention to understand their perspective
- Validate their feelings and viewpoint (this does not mean you agree)
- Ask them what they need
- Let them know they aren't alone

There are plenty more to list, but to keep it simple, just remember to show up with an intention to support their underlying issue. This does not mean you condone *the behavior* or that they are "getting away with it." Having this connection with them will give them hope that they can be more successful and they'll be more willing to work with you. If they have someone in their corner, they will be much more receptive to engage in the next crucial step towards taking ownership of their actions.

2. Reflect for Growth

Once trust is built and the student has regulated their emotions, the brain's frontal cortex is activated, and the student can think more rationally. This sets the stage for a more productive conversation in which the student has a chance to take responsibility for their negative behavior, discover the reason for the misbehavior, and explore next steps. We'll cover damage repair next in Step 3. For now, let's focus on how we can stimulate growth and behavior change.

Many times in secondary schools, we assume that because our students are tall or have facial hair and look like young adults, they possess the skills needed to succeed. We assume they will change their behavior after processing the impact of their actions. Unfortunately, many students don't have the capacity to do this well, or have limited reflection skills, due to a lack of practice, knowledge, instruction, brain structure, or experience.

We need to serve as the gatekeepers to guide them through the reflection process. We need to show them *how* to reflect upon their choices and actions and decide how they are going to make reparations. To address this, we lead a reflection activity, regardless of the severity of the infraction,[38] which includes a series of questions for the student to answer after engaging in unhealthy behavior. This can be administered verbally or in writing. It's meant for them to consider how their actions may affect their own life and impact others.

Asking meaningful reflection questions will help motivate these kids with more of an internal drive and foster introspection. Now let's look at how to help them connect back to others they offended or violated so they can feel more confident in re-engaging.

3. Plan to Restore

Any harm done to a relationship, property, situation, etc. needs to be repaired.[39] One of the major flaws regarding ISS or OSS is that it doesn't allow the restoration of what was harmed, such as the relationship between the student and teacher. We suggest using "Relationship Circles," another R.A.T.s team creation, to facilitate these conversations. They ask:

---

[38] Designed by the R.A.T.s group.

[39] National Educators for Restorative Practices. (n.d.). https://stephen-murray-nedrp.squarespace.com/cttreatmentagreement

1. What occurred?
2. Who or what was harmed?
3. Who was impacted by your actions?
4. How do we fix what was broken or harmed?

This conversation first takes place with the student responsible for the misbehavior and then with others who were involved. For example, Mr. O'Brien, an assistant principal we worked with, had a 7th grade student, Nathan, sent to his office after stealing a book from the book fair. In a traditional model, Nathan would have been sent to ISS. Instead of this approach, we decided to use a Relationship Circle to facilitate the conversation, determine how to fix the problem, and guide the desired behaviors. We made some interesting discoveries and devised a plan. Here's how that went:

What occurred?
Nathan stole the book to brag to his peers and gain their approval. He had the money to buy the book but thought he'd gain social status by stealing it.

Who or what was harmed?
The librarian because it took money away from her fundraiser and program.

Who else was impacted by the student's actions?
Other students witnessed the behavior, which may have encouraged them to steal from the book fair, too.

How do we fix what was broken or harmed?
Nathan decided to volunteer at the book fair for two weeks. He thought that sacrificing his time would show the librarian he meant he was truly sorry. He stocked books, looked out for other students who may try to steal, helped direct student traffic, and greeted customers at the door.

Through this process, Nathan had time to reflect on how his decision impacted others and how to repay what was taken. In addition, the relationship between the student and the librarian was repaired, and by the end of the consequence, it was even stronger due to the time they spent together. The time Nathan spent serving as a volunteer was far more impactful than sitting quietly in a room for eight hours.

These strategies align with restorative and trauma-informed practices, which are highly regarded in the school mental health arena. An example of this comes from a report by McInerney & Amy McKlindon (2014) that showed high school suspensions decrease by 83% and expulsions by 40% in the year after implementation of restorative and trauma informed strategies.[40] Finding strategies that easily fit into your school practices and culture are essential for behavior intervention.

Creating Personalized Behavior Action Plans

When we look at the academic tools, resources, and strategies used to help students understand and master subject content, we can see a vast supply of differentiated learning material. When we look at student discipline, the choices of strategy and resources of support dwindle drastically. Similar to an Individualized Education Plan (IEP), designed for academic success, a Personalized Behavior Action Plan (PBAP) is a wonderful tool to:

- customize a plan for improved behavior
- communicate consistently with the support team
- create clear obtainable goals

Below is a story demonstrating the execution of the PBAP tool.

---

[40] McInerney & Amy McKlindon (December 2014). *"Unlocking the door to learning: Trauma-Informed classrooms and transformational schools"* article.

> One afternoon, a 9th grade student, Landon, got in a verbal altercation with another student, which stemmed from the students participating in "Your mama" jokes. Landon became so enraged that he yelled, "Well, tomorrow, I'm going to have my gang beat your ass and then we will see what's up!"
>
> Of course, this caused quite the stir in the classroom, and Landon was sent to the front office. After calling district student services regarding the incident, police officers were also brought in to investigate. The principal called the parents to let them know what occurred, and they assured him that Landon wasn't in a gang.
>
> What should the consequence be for the student?
>
> - ISS or OSS?
> - Expulsion?
> - Legal consequences?
>
> After talking with students, parents, the teacher, district administration, and police, it was evident that Landon was not a threat to his peers or the campus due to his lie, and there was no previous history of aggression or violent incidents. During the investigation, they found out that Landon's family was facing some difficulties and needed additional support. The school team quickly devised a personalized action plan which was approved by the police, district student services, and his parents. The personalized action plan allowed Landon to remain in the educational setting without being arrested for an impulsive act.

Morning Meetings One of the most impactful interventions placed in the PBAP is "Morning Meetings." These meetings typically occur prior to the start of school in a variety of locations, such as teacher classrooms, conference rooms, administrator's office, or counselor's office. This is a quick intervention to provide quality time with students and to gain important information prior to the day starting.

This strategy can be used with any K-12 student, and they are not required to have an Individualized Education Program (IEP) or a 504 plan. Morning Meetings create an opportunity for a trusted adult to have a one-on-one conversation with a troubled student to:

- ask how they're feeling
- identify any needed resource(s)
- assess their mental status

Too often, students go through a high stress event at home (the night before or morning of school), setting them up to be emotionally charged and on edge to start their day. Morning Meetings allow a campus adult to assess the student and determine if they need any resources. Even though this practice is an additional support in the morning, it's a proactive strategy to set the student up for success. It is instrumental in alleviating future escalating student behavior or negative interactions, and uncovers a variety of student needs in advance of the academic day.

School-Based Therapy Many of our students have experienced complex forms of hardship and suffering, and they don't know how to identify their emotions, self-regulate, successfully integrate with their peers, or self-advocate and communicate their needs to an adult. Any one of these is the likely reason for all those classroom disruptions you're experiencing.

Providing time and space for these students onsite with a licensed therapist can help them learn coping skills that directly impact their learning and behavior in both the school and home environment. When we bring a therapist into the school, it removes the barrier of transportation and provides the student an outlet for any bottled-up emotions. School Based Therapists serve as an extension of support for the work your team is already doing. Mostly, it gives kids hope that we care about them and believe they are valuable enough to get them the help they need to thrive.

Social Skills Training Two prevalent areas of youth skill deficiencies include:

1. appropriately interacting in social situations and
2. responding to stress, conflict, or discomfort

Providing time for students to learn and practice their social skills enhances their success, not only in their current situation, but for their entire life. When looking at future in-demand skills and the qualities needed to perform well in the workforce, desirable skills include:

- communication
- emotional intelligence
- collaboration
- social influence
- critical thinking[41]

Some of these skills are taught in the classroom or, perhaps, advisory programs. Often, however, older students, especially in high school, are expected to be proficient in these skills. Of course, not all students are, though, and they need just as much guidance as our little ones do, just in different ways.

We suggest incorporating more skill-building for all students, so they can confidently navigate this complex world successfully. In fact, it

---

[41] Marr, B. (2023, February 14). *The top 10 in-demand skills for 2030.* Forbes. https://www.forbes.com/sites/bernardmarr/2023/02/14/the-top-10-in-demand-skills-for-2030/

would be best to show teachers how to integrate these skills into their teaching practice. Methods to equip teachers include:

- deliver workshops targeting specific skills
- host fun events like a virtual summit
- share recorded bite-sized learning sessions
- teach sessions virtually in special cohorts

Academic Tutoring Oftentimes, outbursts in the classroom and other misbehavior is due to an insecurity with the content, subject matter, or the learning process. Offering students an opportunity to receive additional tutoring from a peer or a teacher allows the student to make academic gains with personalized instruction. We noticed that once they receive support without their peers around, the behaviors are alleviated in many cases.

Health Checks Unfortunately, due to many circumstances at home, a student may need to have occasional or weekly health checks with the school nurse. In our practice with past health checks, we uncovered a whole host of issues that caused frustration, discomfort, or pain, which were able to be treated. The most common areas addressed were vision impairments, seizures, self-harming behaviors, illness, and physical abuse, each of which negatively impacted the learning experience. At-risk children were protected from further harm and referred out for more specialized treatment, too, so taking care of the whole child, rather than solely focusing on academic outcomes, proved to be transformative.

Mentoring Programs We cannot assume every student who walks through our door has a positive support system in their life. When it becomes evident that a student could benefit from working with a trusted adult or peer, as a school, we can provide opportunities to meet with community figures, PTA members, local college students, high school students or a peer. Time with a caring adult or peer gives students a place to discuss what is going on in their world, seek advice, and learn to build a positive and successful relationship while focusing on solutions.

It Isn't Easy As we conclude this section, we'd like you to think about some things before the next disruptive student shows up to your office:

- Is it easy to meet with a student to assess their emotional well-being and determine the "why" behind their actions?
  No, it takes time and energy.
- Is it easy to have a student fix the hurt relationship caused by their actions?
  No, it takes time, energy, and can be emotionally draining.
- Is it easy to determine a unique consequence to teach a student the appropriate behavior in the future?
  No, it takes creativity, time, and effort.

We understand that time, effort, creativity, and emotionality is involved. We understand that change can be hard. But isn't it even more difficult to continuously be disheartened with a process that produces frustrated kids, overwhelmed teachers, and irate parents? If what you're doing is working well, great! Keep it up! If it isn't, we ask that you rally your team and consider a new approach. Continuing to use traditional discipline models and having everyone upset when the student returns with the same behaviors is not likely the goal of anyone involved. We ask that leaders consider putting the time and effort into the set up. Ultimately, we'll always suggest doing what's best for kids.

Take Action

1. Assess your current discipline model.
   The first step in this important work is to assess the current discipline structure in place to see if the steps outlined are assisting in the growth of students' academic, emotional, and behavioral needs. If the answer is "no," it is imperative that the leadership team determine what changes are needed to improve the current student discipline system.

2. Determine if it's best for kids.
   The second step is asking, "Is this discipline method or punishment best for the student and supporting their development, or are we using it because it's easier for the adults involved?"

Some of the traditional ways we are currently handling behavior issues, such as ISS and OSS, are like placing a piece of tape on an open wound: *It may stop the bleeding for a short period of time, but it doesn't fix the injury.*

When addressing misbehavior, we need to allow the student to reflect on their feelings and actions, take ownership, correct their mistakes, and determine a plan moving forward where the consequence is more effective and incorporates time to teach appropriate behavior.

CHAPTER 6

An Ecosystem of Support

"It takes a village to raise a child, and I choose to be an actively participating member of my village."

−Megan Davis

In order for students to truly thrive, we need to work together to expand the network of support. See the graphic below.

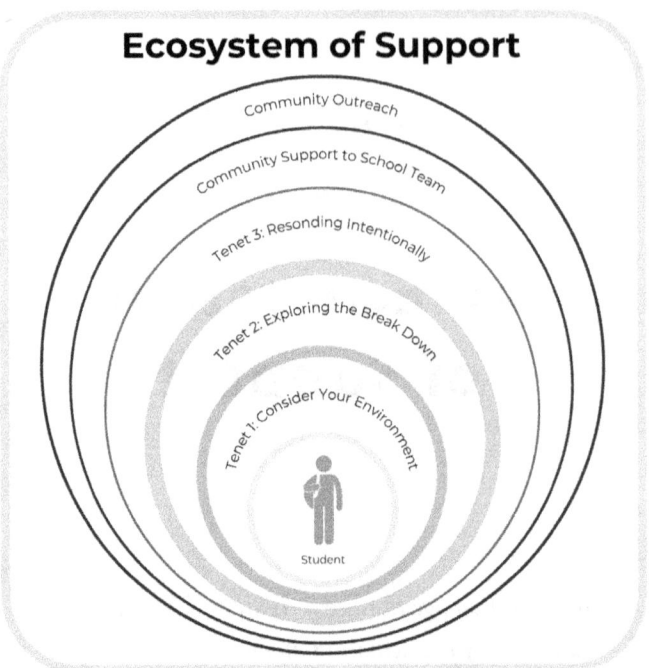

The 3 Tenets provide a framework to meet the needs of students, and expanding outward cultivates a secure ecosystem.

Everyone is on the Team

It takes a cohesive, integrated approach to maintain a well-functioning system. Working in silos breeds inconsistency, so when we aim for stability, it's important to rely on the input and insight from all team members who are equally vested in the goal.

Imagine a concerned parent arriving at the Emergency Room with their young adolescent who is struggling with suicidal ideation. Parents need to know who will be involved in their child's care and how they will help. The whole ordeal can feel chaotic and scary. If the process and communication are clear, however, parents and the patient trust that their child will be OK.

AN ECOSYSTEM OF SUPPORT

There is an intake process where assessments and screenings are conducted to gather important details of the incoming patient's mood, appearance, and description of the incident that landed them there. The treatment team (psychiatrist, therapist, nurse, etc.) convene to discuss the history and behavior patterns, assign a diagnosis, and determine the next best course of action. Each person brings a unique perspective, working together to solve the problem. Essentially, the team's goal is to identify the root cause so they can treat *that* in order to alleviate the symptoms. They administer the plan (therapy, medication, nutrition, etc.) monitor, adjust where necessary, and outline safety measures upon discharge. Everyone on the team contributes, and the parents of the youth are relieved.

A cohesive, viable system must be established in the education system, too. Educators and other faculty members don't have to make a clinical diagnosis, but they're gathering data every day that can aid the team. Typically, there's a disconnect with staff members working in silos. Imagine the outcome for kids when we tighten up communication protocols and processes and address the underlying problem(s) resulting in the misbehavior exhibited by the student. Imagine the relief we'll all get.

Teachers are essential team members. Equipping them with language to effectively share their insights will initiate that network of care. An example of keen insight from a teacher follows:

"Madison has difficulty concentrating during independent work time and seems to zone out when we're having a conversation. She appears sad, flat, and less energetic lately, and she falls asleep during instruction daily. This has been occurring for 2-3 weeks and is not typical for her. I'm concerned."

Rallying the team around students when implementing the 3 Tenets fills gaps and reinforces each tenet since no one is ever working alone. Teachers no longer feel like they're on an island and will trust their student's behavior issue isn't solely on them to address. This ecosystem of support is intended to actually prevent behaviors so there should be a reduction of referrals.

School Mental Health Audit

To start or strengthen our ecosystem of support, we implement the audit. It's a tool to use with the administrative team and other staff who can provide insight into how the system of support is working, based on strengths and weaknesses. Some sections of the audit include:

- School Climate
- Protocols and Practices
- Legal and Ethical Areas
- Communication

Team members can explore areas of strength and identify the most immediate need. This is a way to start the communication process, not fix all that is broken. It doesn't have to be onerous to assess strengths and deficits of our current school mental health system. However, if we're not having these conversations regularly with our leadership staff, we may be missing gaps or barriers that are necessary for maintaining continuity. The School Mental Health Audit also seeks information relating to:

- Staff satisfaction
- Student engagement
- Parent involvement
- Community perception

We start with one area at a time and determine the most pressing need. For example, teachers at a school we worked with were concerned about students who were falling behind or not showing up. Teachers had little, if any, mental health training and were disheartened that no plan was in place to help these kids. We initiated an audit with administrators and determined that the next course of action needed was to provide teachers with a simple plan to assess students and refer them to a point person who would connect these students to a community resource. This provided relief to teachers who now felt like they were getting kids support and did not feel alone in the process. Students were no longer getting left behind, and teachers felt like valued members of the support team.

Discipline Data as a Guiding Tool

It is imperative that the discipline data is not only recorded and assessed but also shared with the entire staff, while also maintaining confidentiality relating to personal student information. Typically, the administrative team compiles data to share with staff in monthly faculty meetings and sometimes in more specialized Positive Behavioral Interventions and Supports (PBIS) meetings. The following categories get tracked and disseminated to the teachers and faculty monthly:

- The total number of infractions
- The level of severity per infraction
- The number of referred students
- The number of repeat offenders
- The number of incidents by grade level

Gauging Progress

A brief review of the data keeps teaching staff linked to the plan and lets them know they are valued members of the team. It's also a great opportunity to think about student behaviors differently and reinforce the use of the 3 Tenets. For staff members resistant to change, this data helps, especially when we emphasize areas of improvement. For those who were onboard from the start, it reinforces their dedication to the process. When assessing the impact of the 3 Tenets, consider the input from all sources and ask:

> Who's looking at the data?
> When is it reviewed?
> What do the results tell us?
> What is working well?
> Where are the gaps?
> What else do we need to know?

Remember Jacob from our introduction? Imagine the opportunity we'd have to prevent a recurrence by asking these kinds of questions. We could make it even easier and train teachers to use the Rapid Research tool and the Cycle of Escalation.

AN ECOSYSTEM OF SUPPORT

For youth who are struggling more than others and may be seeing a school-based therapist or other mental health professional, we can establish regular Check Ins to assess progress toward their goals. This, coupled with regular communication among staff and parents, helps strengthen that ecosystem of support.

Mapping Success with Monthly Results and Evolution

We monitor progress and goal completion using the following tools:

Behavior Metric Take note of a student's behavioral baseline, including an assessment of their current behaviors and emotional state, for future comparison. Define clear success metrics around behavior improvement and emotional well-being benchmarks. Examples:

- behavior logs
- incident reports
- student self-reports

Consider the student's IEP, 504 plan, and any other formal assessment provided by a primary care physician or specialist, assuming there is a Release of Information (ROI). Ultimately, this is a snapshot of the student's decisions, behaviors, and emotional and mental status.

Feedback Loops To receive additional information, incorporate consistent feedback from teachers, students, and parents to determine if adjustments are needed in the plan or goals and additional strategies are required. We use the feedback loop to ensure regular follow up with involved parties such as the teacher(s), admin, student, parent, school counselor, etc. and so that the student receives continued support.

If we think of Jacob as a struggling student, he may avoid engaging in his classes and make excuses to get out of them to roam the hallways. He may participate in Mrs. Franklin's history class, but not in Mr. Ramirez's math class. The Feedback Loop would be helpful in this case because the teachers could share ideas about ways to engage Jacob and how one strategy might work for him better than another. The Feedback Loop is a great way to reiterate what is in the plan, what is working, and what may need to be adjusted for the student's continued success with a behavior plan.

Monthly Review Meetings Convene regular meetings with staff to review and discuss the data collected, student challenges, successes, and next steps in the plan. Communication is key to make sure all stakeholders understand the plan and are consistent in each step.

Digital Surveys & Tools Use simple online surveys or feedback platforms to gather input from teachers, students, and parents regularly. Tools like Google Forms, SurveyMonkey, or Microsoft Forms allow for easy customization and quick distribution, while gaining important and regular feedback from your stakeholders.

Feedback Committees Establish a small group or committee representing teachers, students, and parents who meet periodically to review the plan and provide actionable insights. This reduces wasted time, large-scale feedback efforts, and breakdowns in communication.

Scheduled Check-ins Integrate short feedback check-ins to review data, update on progress, and assign next steps to staff, parents, or students. Using the Feedback Collection Spreadsheet (see below) is important to record all aspects of the check-in communication and action steps.

Data Analysis Software Utilize software that automatically tracks and analyzes student behavior trends. This can help school leaders quickly see patterns and make data-driven decisions on needed adjustments.

Actionable Reporting Regularly communicate key findings and updates to all stakeholders so they feel involved in the process, and ensure they see how their participation in the process leads to positive changes.

Feedback Collection Spreadsheet Example:

Date	Feedback Source	Feedback Method	Feedback Summary	Category (Positive/Constructive)	Action Needed?	Action Assigned To	Follow-Up Date	Status of Follow-Up
10/05/24	Teacher (Mrs. Smith)	Survey (Google Form)	Students struggle with homework comprehension	Constructive	Yes	Curriculum Coordinator	10/15/24	Pending
10/06/24	Parent (Mr. Doe)	Email	Positive feedback on parent-teacher communication	Positive	No	N/A	N/A	Resolved
10/07/24	Student (John Lee)	In-person check-in	Difficulty concentrating in noisy environment	Constructive	Yes	Facilities Manager	10/12/24	In Progress
10/08/24	Teacher (Ms. Garcia)	Survey (Google Form)	Need for professional development on trauma-informed practices	Constructive	Yes	PD Coordinator	10/20/24	Scheduled

Take Action

1. Assess your campus by asking these questions:

   + Do you have a mental health team?
   + Does everyone have a clear role? What is it?
   + How often do you meet?
   + Do you have a central way of communicating?
   + Who else needs to be invited to participate?
   + How do you collect and track student behavior?
   + How do you communicate with outside practitioners who can provide valuable insight?

2. Take a good look at who you currently rely on for mental health issues in your building, and consider who else may need to be a part of the team. Ensure there is a clear communication process and any tools you're using are easily accessible. Reviews should be regular so the team has a place to voice concerns or receive updates on progress and assign a point person to communicate with staff so they know the ecosystem of support is effective.

3. Make a plan to train teachers on using brief intervention strategies, such as the Rapid Research tool, or providing them with some basic knowledge in bite-size form, like the Cycle of Escalation.

CHAPTER 7

Addressing Setbacks

"I never lose. I either win, or I learn."

–Nelson Mandela

Even when there's a strong ecosystem of support, there will be setbacks. Though we might see progress, we're working with kids and teens who will have "off" days. That doesn't mean the whole plan is derailed and that the system shuts down. When something goes wrong, review the circumstances, note any complications or new issues that arise, and develop strategies to overcome them to ensure continual improvement. Most importantly, accept that disruption is a normal part of change, and the way we respond will influence the level of trust and school climate. Openly recognizing the setback is an important validation to whom it affected, and it's an opportunity for modeling forward motion and problem-solving through adversity. Below are strategies for maintaining stability and handling setbacks.

Team Check Ins

In the last chapter, we asked you to assemble your Mental Health Team and establish a simple system of communication and review of progress. Now we need to focus on adapting to adversity in order to maintain a stable ecosystem of support. Conduct regular Check Ins and Check Outs with your team. Here are some important questions to use in this process:

Check Ins
What is working *now*?
What worked in the *past*?
What is currently *missing*?

Team Check In

- What is working now?
- What worked in the past?
- What is missing?

We typically focus on the negative aspects of change, but what happens if we embrace change when we know it will result in what is best for kids? In the past, we often found that we needed to take a step back in order to take a step forward. There are always roadblocks that can make implementation difficult. Below is an example of how the "check-in" process can work with the Mental Health Team as they reflect on an individual student:

> One of our students, when faced with any adversity in their day, would have fight or flight tendencies. As teachers and administrators began to build a relationship with the student, they uncovered that the student's parents were going through a difficult divorce due to alcoholism and the environment at home was very chaotic. Based on the behaviors being exhibited at school, a behavior plan was constructed. As the Mental Health Team met to conduct a check-in on this student, the following questions were considered:
>
> *What is working now?*
> - *The student was showing success with the following strategies:*
> - *Take mental health breaks during class.*
> - *Meeting with a district counselor each week.*
> - *Participating in an after school extracurricular activity.*
>
> *What worked in the past?*
> Previously, the student would participate in a morning check-in with the assistant principal prior to their first period class.
>
> *What is missing?*
> Since the morning check-in was removed from the student's plan, the team has noticed an increase in negative behaviors. The Mental Health Team is recommending that the student participate in a one-on-one check-in with a "trusted" adult. It is obvious the student found the personalized time beneficial to their mental health.

This is one of many examples where there seemed to be an easy solution to a set of behavior problems; however, if you don't have a team constructed and/or you don't have a reflective process established, it will be difficult to identify the solutions, determine changes in the plan, and communicate to all staff involved.

Stay clear and focused, and let the 3 Tenets guide you. Follow Nelson Mandela's advice shared in the quote above as a mantra if that's helpful. Remember this when trying to make an impact on your own campus or with your students. Even when you are met with challenges, consider all you've learned, resort back to the three questions we posed, and don't give up.

Withstanding Changes

In all aspects of life, change is inevitable. As we mentioned, how we adapt to the change makes the difference between chaos and calm. New leaders will be appointed, staff will turnover, political and social climates will ebb and flow, and policies will evolve as our world changes. Even with the best intentions and people in power, there will be failed initiatives from time to time. Having the 3 Tenets in place will withstand vacillation if used consistently and collectively.

Staff Turnover

The National Association of Secondary School Principals (NASSP) and the Learning Policy Institute at Stanford University found that nearly one in five principals leave their school each year, with the average building leader's tenure lasting about four years.[42] With a building

---

[42] National Association of Secondary School Principals (NASSP). (2023, April 24). *With nearly half of principals considering leaving, research urges attention to working conditions, compensation, and supports.*

ADDRESSING SETBACKS

leadership change, many aspects of the campus culture, policy, procedures, and initiatives change, too. By infusing the 3 Tenets into school structures and embedding them as core practices of the entire school community, it will ensure longevity, despite inevitable staff turnover. The fabric of the 3 Tenets are rooted in the system design and continue to integrate into classroom instruction, team plans, reparation procedures, alternative consequence constructs, and the design of safe physical spaces. Maintaining the staff who initiate the 3 Tenets, communicating the "why" behind the existence of the systems to new leadership, and providing successful data, will allow the practices to remain and live beyond leadership change.

Similar to leadership turnover, teacher transfers, retirement, promotions, and other staffing situations are inevitable. When onboarding new staff, setting them up to learn the systems early and reinforcing the 3 Tenets will ensure a smoother transition.

Once the 3 Tenets are a part of the campus culture and standard practice, the initiative will continue. Remember, if an initiative remains a priority, it will withstand change. So the questions to ask here are:

1. Do you have a clear and simple onboarding process?

If **yes**, great! How are new staff guided through it and where can they seek help if they get stuck? If **not**, what's missing, or what would make it easier for new staff to get acclimated to your policies, procedures, and culture?

2. How do staff members incorporate the 3 Tenets? Where do they start, and who will lead them?
3. How do we know staff have adjusted well? Who will check in with them, and how will they confirm they are getting their needs met?

Budget Cuts and Resource Limitations

Many schools have experienced a consistent reduction in funding at the state and district level for professional development, mental health support, and added staff, such as counselors, administrators, teachers, and social workers. With the 3 Tenets established, additional funding does provide more support but is not needed for systems to run effectively. Let's take a look at each Tenet in regard to budget:

Tenet 1: Consider Your Environment
Simple changes to the physical environment, like rearranging furniture to encourage collaboration, decluttering classrooms, or adding natural light, can foster a sense of calm and order without significant monetary investments. Looking at the implementation of the social and emotional strategies, such as daily greetings, mindfulness moments, or movement breaks, require time and intentionality, not extra funding.

Tenet 2: Explore the Break Down
Understanding the root causes of student behavior provides a framework for responding effectively, even when additional resources (e.g., counselors or social workers) are limited. When resources are tight, schools can establish peer-led support teams, mental health teams, and mentor groups to address challenges collaboratively without requiring additional funding.

Tenet 3: Respond Intentionally
In the absence of ample resources, responding intentionally ensures that educators are meeting students' core needs and addressing behavior constructively, without unnecessary strain on staff or systems. Training staff to avoid power struggles costs nothing but can significantly reduce conflict and improve relationships between students and educators. In addition, creating teacher-led teams, such as the Relationship Action Team or Push-In Core Team, to focus on improving connections and

relationships with students, ensures everyone is supported without needing outside professionals.

Political and Social Climates

The political climate across the nation and around the world has become intense and, often, polarizing. Policies relating to public education can cause strong emotions among stakeholders. Everyone has an opinion, and it seems most people have the best intention for kids in mind (we hope), but as long as adults remain at odds about best educational practices, students will likely suffer the consequences. Sometimes concepts with plenty of data to support their efficacy, like "trauma," and social emotional learning (SEL), become politicized and cast aside.

This instability will show up everywhere, so instead of waiting for adults to play nice, we're asking leaders to put their energy into strengthening the connection among the people *within* the systems to improve their own school culture, regardless of the battles occurring on the perimeter. We support advocacy, sure. (We'll get to that in the next section). But, while the adults are sorting out the details, we want to be certain about protecting our students. With the 3 Tenets as a guide, and a move towards discipline methods that teach appropriate behavior and support our most vulnerable youth, we will withstand these societal shifts and conflicts.

Lack of Celebrating Successes

Although this is, perhaps, the most important step, it is one that is most often forgotten. We need to take time to acknowledge and praise student (and staff) achievements and improvements as a way to boost morale and motivate staff to continue with the plan. After all, valuable time and effort at this point has gone into the plan, so calling out the wins, both large and small, will go a long way towards maintaining momentum. However, celebrating success need not require grand gestures or a great deal of time. Indeed, celebrations can be as simple as:

- Positive phone calls home
- Sticky notes of praise
- A printed certificate
- An added privilege
- A small token, like a sticker or coffee

Positive reinforcement will encourage and motivate the student (or staff member) to continue the behavior and build positive habits moving forward.

Take Action

Take the first step by initiating a Team Check-In. Start by incorporating it into your Monthly Meetings to foster consistent reflection and growth, or use it as needed to evaluate and refine processes or procedures that could benefit from adjustment. This simple action can pave the way for meaningful progress and alignment within your team.
As you conduct your Team Check-Ins, don't forget the importance of celebrating achievements along the way.

Recognizing and praising both student and staff improvements, no matter how big or small, boosts morale and motivates everyone to stay engaged with the plan. Incorporate celebrations into your campus culture by weaving them into team check-ins, monthly meetings, or day-to-day interactions. A positive phone call home, a handwritten sticky note of praise, a small token of appreciation like a sticker or coffee, or even a school-wide initiative like a "Wall of Achievements" can go a long way in creating a supportive, uplifting environment. By embedding celebrations into your regular practices, you not only recognize individual success but also foster a culture of positivity, connection, and shared growth that drives continued progress across your campus.

CHAPTER 8

A Move Toward Change

"In any given moment, we have two options: to step forward into growth or step back into safety."

–Abraham Maslow

The language of behavior is one we all need to learn. As we band together to nurture children, teens, and young adults into more independent beings, interpreting their behavior provides us the insight needed to navigate challenges more effectively. When we learn *their* language and respond in ways *they* interpret as trusting and secure, we guide them into adulthood with more success.

Protective Factors

In social work, we identify protective factors (positive influences) in various environments to keep kids secure and stabilized. Examples of protective factors:[43] [44]

- Supervision
- Social supports
- Stable housing
- Food security
- Good health
- Problem-solving skills
- Self-esteem
- Academic success
- Reliable transportation

If we can establish these in advance, prior to an incident, and form a strong interconnected system around students, they have more stable environments to move between. This impacts their wellbeing and ability to thrive. "Targeting only one context when addressing a person's risk or protective factors is unlikely to be successful, because people don't exist in isolation."[45] That's why we need to implement the 3 Tenets *everywhere*.

---

[43] https://www.publicsafety.gc.ca/cnt/cntrng-crm/crm-prvntn/fndng-prgrms/rsk-fctrs-en.aspx

[44] https://www.samhsa.gov/sites/default/files/20190718-samhsa-risk-protective-factors.pdf

[45] Illinois University Library. (n.d.). *Social factors and drug use.*

Adaptability Across Settings

We can learn to translate behavior in any setting, within any context, under any circumstances using the 3 Tenets. This will help us develop more stable parents, loving partners, productive employees, effective managers, critical thinkers, and articulate communicators. The 3 Tenets are purposefully designed to adapt across diverse settings to cultivate more protective factors around youth, which is why it's crucial to implement them in varied settings. As we conclude this book, we'll show you how to apply this new framework in varied environments to get you started.

Educators

As we have mentioned in earlier chapters, we believe educators have a duty to share the responsibility of child-rearing since kids gather in schools outside of the home in the masses (remember the benefits of community). Educators can make a major impact when they have more intentionality about their environment, response plan, and systems of support. We have been teaching kids SEL skills in school settings, though it isn't enough to solve the underlying behavior issues we're seeing because the adults are not fully equipped. Classrooms are, of course, a natural learning environment as well, so we need to integrate the 3 Tenets there.

Subsequently, teachers will feel less strain and more confidence when armed with a simplified process to reframe a potentially escalating situation with a student. In fact, they can prevent conflict in the first place and will be energized to teach with more enthusiasm. Imagine the outcome Jacob might have if his teachers implemented the 3 Tenets in their practice. It extends beyond the classroom as a whole-building approach. Instead of feeling defensive and escalating his behavior, Jacob may feel heard, accepted, and cared for while having a plan for increased success. He may engage more in his classes and build trusting relationships with his teachers. A student like Jacob may have an entirely different school experience that transforms from a negative perspective into a positive one.

Families

We're not giving families an "out" by accepting a shared responsibility in our schools. Rather, we form strong bonds and build the partnerships so desperately needed to form allies without our communities around our children. We need to rely upon each other and trust that each of us plays a vital role in influencing their character.

Typically, we place the blame and burden on parents when our students misbehave. Though they absolutely play a critical role and do have responsibility in correcting and guiding their children's behavior, we're suggesting that we look more holistically at the family system. What are all the factors contributing to the behavior? Can other family members meet the child's needs where their parents are lacking? Can grandparents, aunts/uncles, adult siblings, foster parents, and other caregivers connected to our kids contribute? It's time we support the immensely challenging position parents face and send a message that we're all in this together.

Organizations

How many different roles do adults fill in our school buildings, organizations, and extracurricular events? For instance:

- Coaches
- Volunteers
- Custodians

- Bus drivers
- Front office
- Cross guards
- Para Educators
- Advisors

Kids encounter these people every day, so equipping them with tools to respond more effectively to our children's needs will have a profound impact on the way they learn and experience their culture.

Workplace

Business owners invest in a workforce to increase productivity, efficiency, revenue, and innovation. When their employees or contractors do not perform optimally, however, it can have devastating effects on their goals.

Incorporating the 3 Tenets into our workplace practice can have lasting, positive results since we are investing in human capital. Equipping employees and company leaders with these tools and strategies will strengthen their ability to relate to others and better meet their needs. Implementation of the 3 Tenets will benefit:

- Customer service
- Communication
- Issue resolution
- Strategic planning
- Employee wellness

Society is changing, and we desperately need solid workers using critical thinking, making reasonable decisions, and feeling energized to perform well.

Generational Change

As we support educators throughout the country, the number one thing we hear from administrators and teachers is, "The kids have changed." And you know what? They are right. The students we serve have gone through a great deal over the past several years, including a national pandemic, political hate, racial inequity, book banning, and an increase on the reliance of technology.

In addition to the societal strife, chronic stress, and trauma, we have now been through at least one full generation of students who were taught to be critical and independent thinkers. We encouraged them to stand up for their rights, protect their bodies, and advocate for each other. Kids *are* using the skills we taught them and *have* moved beyond automatic obedience and compliance that traditional education and parenting systems emphasized in previous generations.

In the movie *A Star is Born*, the talented Bradley Cooper sings a song with the chorus, "Maybe it's time to let the old ways die."[46] It challenges us to push through social traditions when change feels difficult. This question is perfect for the world of education and, specifically, with solutions to student behavior. We understand the need to teach and guide children along their journey into adulthood, though traditional approaches will continue to cause friction because societal norms have simply changed.

Learning the language of today's youth will help us better understand how to respond to behavior and meet their needs. Ultimately, we'd like to enjoy the child-rearing process and produce healthier, sustainable outcomes for future generations to come.

So as we conclude, please ask yourself: *What traditional student behavior practices need to be eliminated and how can you be the answer to the needed change?* You have the power to positively impact so many

---

[46] *A Star Is Born*. Directed by Bradley Cooper, performances by Bradley Cooper and Lady Gaga, Warner Bros. Pictures, 2018.

students' educational experiences and, with the use of the 3 Tenets, transform a child's life forever.

Take Action

We know that dealing with student misbehavior is a real struggle. You may feel angry, disheartened, and defeated by your current situation, but know this: you have everything you need, and all the right tools, to make the change you wish to see. You chose this work with a burning desire to set kids up for a successful future. The 3 Tenets offer a framework to not only support your students but to reignite your passion for your role in education.

We encourage you to focus on manageable first steps rather than trying to implement everything at once. Progress comes from consistent, small actions. You don't need to have all the answers or make sweeping changes overnight. Start with one tenet, one strategy, or even one positive student interaction, and let the momentum build naturally. Here are three easy action steps to start with:

- Choose one student with whom you'd like to build a stronger relationship.
- Identify one new strategy to implement within the next week.
- Share your experience with a colleague or reflect in a journal.

With consistency and practice, these strategies will become a daily norm that are embedded in your classroom or campus culture. You *will* make a difference! We want you to know that you are not alone in this work. Change happens through collaboration. When teachers, counselors, administrators, support staff, and other community partners work together, the impact is exponential. Just imagine a school where every student feels seen, valued, and capable of success. By taking action, one step at a time, you're not just changing behaviors, you're transforming lives. We believe in you and your ability to inspire others.

References

A Star Is Born. Directed by Bradley Cooper, performances by Bradley Cooper and Lady Gaga, Warner Bros. Pictures, 2018.

Allday, R. A., & Pakurar, K. (2007). Effects of teacher greetings on student on-task behavior. *Journal of applied behavior analysis*, 40(2), 317–320. https://doi.org/10.1901/jaba.2007.86-06

American Psychological Association Zero Tolerance Task Force. (2008). Zero tolerance policies: An issue brief. *American Psychologist*, 63(9), 852–862. https://doi.org/10.1037/0003-066X.63.9.852

Balfanz, R., & Boccanfuso, C. (2007). Falling off the path of graduation: Early indicators brief. Graduation Center.

Berkman, E. T. (2018). The Neuroscience of Goals and Behavior Change. *Consulting psychology journal*, 70(1), 28–44. https://doi.org/10.1037/cpb0000094

Bersia M, Koumantakis E, Berchialla P, Charrier L, Ricotti A, Dalmasso P, et al. Suicide spectrum among young people in early phases of the COVID-19 pandemic: a systematic review and meta-analysis. eClinicalMedicine. (2022) 54:101705. 10.1016/j.eclinm.2022.101705

Center for Disease Control and Prevention (CDC). https://www.cdc.gov/violenceprevention/aces/about.html

Center for Substance Abuse Treatment (US). Trauma-Informed Care in Behavioral Health Services. Rockville (MD): Substance Abuse and Mental Health Services Administration (US); 2014. (Treatment Improvement Protocol (TIP) Series, No. 57.) Chapter 3, Understanding the Impact of Trauma. Available from: https://www.ncbi.nlm.nih.gov/books/NBK207191/

Chang, Cindy. (2006, April 2). *Cool Tat, Too Bad It's Gibberish*. The New York Times. https://www.nytimes.com/2006/04/02/fashion/sundaystyles/cool-tat-too-bad-its-gibberish.html

Collaborative for Academic, Social, and Emotional Learning (CASEL). (2007, December). *Background on Social Emotional Learning (SEL)*. University of Illinois at Chicago. https://files.eric.ed.gov/fulltext/ED505362.pdf

Copeland, W. E., Keeler, G., Angold, A., & Costello, E. J. (2007). Traumatic events and posttraumatic stress in childhood. *Archives of General Psychology, 64*, 577–584.

Costello, B. (2009). *The restorative practices handbook: For teachers, disciplinarians, and administrators*. International Institute for Restorative Practices.

Echo. (2019). *We love science: the physical impact of trauma*. https://www.echotraining.org/we-love-science/

Greene, R., W. (2024, April 8). *What are the lagging skills holding your child back?* ADDitude. https://www.additudemag.com/lagging-skills-unsolved-problems-alsup/

Haidt, Jonathan. (2023, June 6). *The Case for Phone-Free Schools*. https://www.afterbabel.com/p/phone-free-schools?r=182klo&utm_campaign=post&utm_medium=email

Hairston, Stephanie. (2019, July 11). *How Grief Shows Up in Your Body*. Web MD. https://www.webmd.com/special-reports/grief-stages/20190711/how-grief-affects-your-body-and-mind#:~:text=Stress%20links%20the%20emotional%20,easily%20as%20physical%20threats%20can

Hannigan, J. D., & Hannigan, J. E. (2022). *Don't Suspend Me!* (2nd ed.). Corwin Publishing.

Hattie, J. (n.d.). *Hattie ranking: Influences and effect sizes related to student achievement*. Visible Learning. Retrieved October 10, 2024, from https://visible-learning.org/hattie-ranking-influences-effect-sizes-learning-achievement/

HeartMath Institute Research Staff, (2016). *The Science Behind the Heartmath System*.

Hunt, Tenah K.A., Slack, Kristen S., Berger, Lawrence M. (2017). Adverse childhood experiences and behavioral problems in middle childhood. https://www.sciencedirect.com/science/article/abs/pii/S0145213416302563

REFERENCES

Illinois University Library. (n.d.). *Social factors and drug use*. In *Drug use and misuse: A community health Perspective*. https://iopn.library.illinois.edu/pressbooks/druguseandmisuse/chapter/social-factors-and-drug-use/#:~:text=A%20variety%20of%20risk%20and,don%27t%20exist%20in%20isolation

Jimenez, Kayla. (2023, June 12). *Behavior vs. books: US students are rowdier than ever post-COVID. How's a teacher to Teach?* https://www.usatoday.com/in-depth/news/education/2023/06/12/us-schools-see-behavioral-issues-climb-post-covid/70263874007/

Jovanovic, T., Blanding, N. Q., Norrholm, S. D., Duncan, E., Bradley, B., & Ressler, K. J. (2009). Childhood abuse is associated with increased startle reactivity in adulthood. *Depression and anxiety, 26*(11), 1018–1026. https://doi.org/10.1002/da.20599

Kardiner & Spiegel (1947). https://www.cdc.gov/injury/priority/index.html#:~:text=Having%20any%20ACE%20is%20associated,to%20adults%20with%20no%20ACEs.

Kentucky Department of Education. (n.d.). *Kentucky multi-tiered system of supports (KyMTSS) implementation guide*. Retrieved November 22, 2024, from https://www.education.ky.gov/curriculum/standards/teachtools/Documents/KyMTSS_Implementation_Guide.pdf

Public Safety Canada. (n.d.). *Risk factors for crime and violence*. Retrieved August 10, 2023, from https://www.publicsafety.gc.ca/cnt/cntrng-crm/crm-prvntn/fndng-prgrms/rsk-fctrs-en.aspx

Purvis, K. and Cross, D. (2017). "Trust-Based Relational Intervention". Karen Purvis Institute of Child Development. https://texascasa.org/wp-content/uploads/2023/04/Instructor-Introduction-Overview.pdf

Kentucky Department of Education. (2021, November). Trauma Informed Discipline Response and Behavior System. https://www.education.ky.gov/school/sdfs/Documents/Trauma%20Informed%20Discipline%20Response%20and%20Behavior%20System.pdf

Marr, B. (2023, February 14). *The top 10 in-demand skills for 2030*. Forbes. https://www.forbes.com/sites/bernardmarr/2023/02/14/the-top-10-in-demand-skills-for-2030/

McInerney, M., & McKlindon, A. (2014). Unlocking the door to learning: Trauma-Informed classrooms and transformational schools. Education Law Center. https://www.pacesconnection.com/g/aces-in-education/fileSendAction/fcType/5/fcOid/480528347493407227/fodoid/480528347493407226/TraumaInformed%20Classrooms_Transformational%20Schools_Unlocking%20the%20Door%20to%20Learning_24%20pages.pdf

McMahon, E. M., Hemming, L., Robinson, J., & Griffin, E. (2023). Editorial: Suicide and self harm in young people. *Frontiers in psychiatry, 13*, 1120396. https://doi.org/10.3389/fpsyt.2022.1120396

National Association of Secondary School Principals (NASSP). (2023, April 24). *With nearly half of principals considering leaving, research urges attention to working conditions, compensation, and supports.*

National Educators for Restorative Practices. (n.d.). https://stephen-murray-nedrp.squarespace.com/cttreatmentagreement

Neuroscience News. (2024). *Global Stress and Inflammation: A Cycle of Societal Dysfunction.* https://neurosciencenews-com.cdn.ampproject.org/c/s/neurosciencenews.com/stress-inflammation-cognition-social-25738/amp/

Ohio Department of Education. (2024). Trauma Informed Schools. https://education.ohio.gov/Topics/Student-Supports/School-Wellness/Trauma-Informed-Schools

O'Neill, L., Guenette, F. and Kitchenham, A. (2010), 'Am I safe here and do you like me?' Understanding complex trauma and attachment disruption in the classroom. British Journal of Special Education, 37: 190-197. https://doi.org/10.1111/j.1467-8578.2010.00477.x

Pauketat, R., Wang, E. L., Kaufman, J. H., Gittens, A. D. & Auketat, A. W. (2023). *Teachers' Perceptions of Coherence in K–12 English Language Arts and Mathematics Instructional Systems.* RAND Corporation; Bill & Melinda Gates Foundation. https://www.rand.org/pubs/research_reports/RRA279-3.html

Perna, Mark C. (2024). *No More Teachers: The Epic Crisis Facing Education In 2024.* https://www.forbes.com/sites/markcperna/2024/01/03/no-more-teachers-the-epic-crisis-facing-education-in-2024/?sh=12424fde4736

REFERENCES

Psychology Today Staff. (202). Rejection Sensitivity. https://www.psychologytoday.com/us/basics/rejection-sensitivity?amp

Rampen, D. C., Pangelmanan, A. S., & Mandagi, D. W. (2023). The X-factors behind Gen Z employee performance: A systematic review. 7(2):2685-4236, DOI:10.35335/mantik.v7i2.3919.

Reavis, J. A., Looman, J., Franco, K. A., & Rojas, B. (2013). Adverse childhood experiences and adult criminality: how long must we live before we possess our own lives?. *The Permanente journal, 17*(2), 44–48. https://doi.org/10.7812/TPP/12-072

Siegel, D. J. (Year). *Hand Model of the Brain* [Video]. Retrieved from https://www.youtube.com/watch?v=gm9CIJ74Oxw

Substance Abuse and Mental Health Services Administration (SAMHSA). (2019). Risk and Protective Factors. https://www.samhsa.gov/sites/default/files/20190718-samhsa-risk-protective-factors.pdf

Tanil, C. T., & Yong, M. H. (2020). Mobile phones: The effect of its presence on learning and memory. *PloS one, 15*(8), e0219233. https://doi.org/10.1371/journal.pone.0219233

The Lancet Child Adolescent Health. Adolescent wellbeing in the UK. Lancet Child Adolesc Health. (2021) 5:681. 10.1016/S2352-4642(21)00284-4

Twenge, J. M. (2020). Increases in Depression, Self-Harm, and Suicide Among U.S. Adolescents After 2012 and Links to Technology Use: Possible Mechanisms. Psychiatric Research and Clinical Practice, 2(1), 19–25. https://doi.org/10.1176/appi.prcp.20190015

U.S. Department of Education Office for Civil Rights. (2021). *An overview of exclusionary discipline practices in public schools for the 2017–18 school year* [PowerPoint slides]. https://www2.ed.gov/about/offices/list/ocr/docs/crdc-exclusionary-school-discipline.pdf

Valiente, C., Swanson, J., DeLay, D., Fraser, A. M., & Parker, J. H. (2020). Emotion-related socialization in the classroom: Considering the roles of teachers, peers, and the classroom context. *Developmental psychology, 56*(3), 578–594. https://doi.org/10.1037/dev0000863

van der Kolk, B. (2014). The Body Keeps the Score, Chapter 2.

Wald, J., & Losen, D. (2003). Deconstructing the school-to-prison pipeline: New directions for youth development. Jossey-Bass.

Acknowledgements

Joshua Stamper

I am profoundly grateful to my incredible family, whose unwavering love and support have been the foundation of this journey. To my amazing wife, Leslie, thank you for your endless patience, encouragement, and for standing by me through endless edits with both grace and understanding. To my children, Mila, Landon, Gabriel, Aden, Elijah, and Layla, your curiosity, resilience, and boundless imagination have been my constant inspiration. You remind me every day why this work matters. Thank you all for being my heart and my motivation.

Charle Peck

I am incredibly grateful for my husband, Kyle, who always encourages me and is gracious and tolerant of my ideas and goals. None of this would be possible without his love and genuine belief in me. My children, Nicolas, Jonas, and Grayson, are always my reason for striving for a better future. They light up my soul and remind me of the true meaning of life. Finally, I am so proud of my co-author, Joshua Stamper, who truly inspires everyone who meets him. His trust in me to complete this project will never be forgotten.

About the Authors

Charle Peck is the co-author of *The Language of Behavior*, a framework for behavior prevention and intervention, and co-author of *Improving School Mental Health: The Thriving School Community Solution*, a revolutionary program to optimize student learning outcomes and wellbeing. She holds an MS in Education and an MS in Social Work as a 20+ year veteran in education (K-12). As a global keynote speaker, she delivers powerful messages of hope to educators and facilitates meaningful professional learning sessions to equip adults with tools that integrate into everyday practice. Her unique lens as a high school teacher turned clinical therapist, and her work with adolescents and families in crisis, makes her stories relevant and captivating to those struggling in today's system. You can purchase her books on Amazon and connect with her via her website CharlePeck.com and on LinkedIn @CharlePeck.

Joshua Stamper is a dedicated educator, speaker, author, and creator of *Aspire to Lead*. With a rich background in teaching and school administration, Joshua brings invaluable insight into the challenges and opportunities within the education system. His personal journey as a struggling student, combined with nine years of experience as a middle school administrator, fuels his passion for creating supportive and transformative learning environments. Joshua is committed to helping educators and leaders unlock their full potential, fostering growth, and inspiring lasting change in education.

As co-author of *The Language of Behavior*, Joshua focuses on equipping educators with trauma-responsive strategies and alternative behavior practices to support student success. Through his work, he continues to empower education professionals to lead with empathy, implement innovative approaches, and make a meaningful impact in their schools and communities. Connect with Joshua at: www.JoshStamper.com or email at Joshua@JoshStamper.com

More from ConnectEDD Publishing

Since 2015, ConnectEDD has worked to transform education by empowering educators to become better-equipped to teach, learn, and lead. What started as a small company designed to provide professional learning events for educators has grown to include a variety of services to help educators and administrators address essential challenges. ConnectEDD offers instructional and leadership coaching, professional development workshops focusing on a variety of educational topics, a roster of nationally recognized educator associates who possess hands-on knowledge and experience, educational conferences custom-designed to meet the specific needs of schools, districts, and state/national organizations, and ongoing, personalized support, both virtually and onsite. In 2020, ConnectEDD expanded to include publishing services designed to provide busy educators with books and resources consisting of practical information on a wide variety of teaching, learning, and leadership topics. Please visit us online at connecteddpublishing.com or contact us at: info@connecteddpublishing.com

Recent Publications:

Live Your Excellence: Action Guide by Jimmy Casas

Culturize: Action Guide by Jimmy Casas

Daily Inspiration for Educators: Positive Thoughts for Every Day of the Year by Jimmy Casas

Eyes on Culture: Multiply Excellence in Your School by Emily Paschall

Pause. Breathe. Flourish. Living Your Best Life as an Educator by William D. Parker

L.E.A.R.N.E.R. Finding the True, Good, and Beautiful in Education by Marita Diffenbaugh

Educator Reflection Tips Volume II: Refining Our Practice by Jami Fowler-White

Handle With Care: Managing Difficult Situations in Schools with Dignity and Respect by Jimmy Casas and Joy Kelly

Disruptive Thinking: Preparing Learners for Their Future by Eric Sheninger

Permission to be Great: Increasing Engagement in Your School by Dan Butler

Daily Inspiration for Educators: Positive Thoughts for Every Day of the Year, Volume II by Jimmy Casas

The 6 Literacy Levers: Creating a Community of Readers by Brad Gustafson

The Educator's ATLAS: Your Roadmap to Engagement by Weston Kieschnick

MORE FROM CONNECTEDD PUBLISHING

In This Season: Words for the Heart by Todd Nesloney, LaNesha Tabb, Tanner Olson, and Alice Lee

Leading with a Humble Heart: A 40-Day Devotional for Leaders by Zac Bauermaster

Recalibrate the Culture: Our Why…Our Work…Our Values by Jimmy Casas

Creating Curious Classrooms: The Beauty of Questions by Emma Chiappetta

Crafting the Culture: 45 Reflections on What Matters Most by Joe Sanfelippo and Jeffrey Zoul

Improving School Mental Health: The Thriving School Community Solution by Charle Peck and Dr. Cameron Caswell

Building Authenticity: A Blueprint for the Leader Inside You by Todd Nesloney and Tyler Cook

Connecting Through Conversation: A Playbook for Talking with Kids by Erika Bare and Tiffany Burns

The Dream Factory: Designing a Purposeful Life by Mark Trumbo

Stories Behind Stances: Creating Empathy Through Hearing "The Other Side" by Chris Singleton

Happy Eyes: All Things to All People by Ryan Tillman

The Generative Age Artificial Intelligence and the Future of Education by Alana Winnick

Recalibrate the Culture: Action Guide by Jimmy Casas

Leading with PEOPLE: A Six Pillar Framework for Fruitful Leadership by Zac Bauermaster

THE LANGUAGE OF BEHAVIOR

A School Leader's Guide to Reclaiming Purpose by Frederick C. Buskey

Foundations of an Elite Culture: Building Success with High Standards and a Positive Environment by David Arencibia

Personalize: Meeting the Needs of All Learners by Eric Sheninger and Nicki Slaugh

The Five Principles of Educator Professionalism: Rebuilding Trust in Schools by Nason Lollar

Words on the Wall: Culturizing Your Classroom for Observable Impact by Jimmy Casas and Cale Birk

School of Engagement: 45 Activities to Ignite Student Learning by Jonathan Alsheimer

Intentional Instructional Moves: Strategic Steps to Accelerate Student Learning by Sherry St. Clair

Overcoming Education: Complex Challenges, Difficult People, and the Art of Making a Difference by Brad R. Gustafson

www.ingramcontent.com/pod-product-compliance
Lightning Source LLC
Chambersburg PA
CBHW070627030426
42337CB00020B/3939